Learning to Live
Without Cigarettes

WILLIAM A. ALLEN is a graduate of the University of Minnesota with an undergraduate degree in Journalism. He holds an M.A. degree in Public Health from Minnesota, and served for several years with the Minnesota Department of Health. A past president of the Pennsylvania Public Health Association, he is presently employed as Director of Health Education, Philadelphia Department of Health, and serves as Director of the Philadelphia Smoking and Health Demonstration Project.

GERHARD ANGERMANN received his undergraduate degree from the University of Pennsylvania. From 1953–63, he served as Director of Research in Advanced Studies at the Central High School in Philadelphia. A member of the Philadelphia Advisory Committee on Smoking and Health, Mr. Angermann is presently employed by the Public Health Service as supervisor of the Philadelphia Smoking and Health Project.

WILLIAM A. FACKLER is presently employed by the Public Health Service and the Albert Einstein Medical Center and Moss Rehabilitation Hospital as Administrator-Health Educator of the Pulmonary Unit. A former supervisor of the Philadelphia Smoking and Health Project, he is presently an active member of the National Interagency Council on Smoking and Health. Mr. Fackler received his M.A. degree in Health and Physical Education from the University of Maryland. He is a fellow in the American and Pennsylvania Public Health Associations, and the Society of the Public Health Educators.

# Learning to Live Without Cigarettes

William A. Allen

Gerhard Angermann

William A. Fackler

DOLPHIN BOOKS
DOUBLEDAY & COMPANY, INC.
GARDEN CITY, NEW YORK

The development of the original material in this publication was made possible in part through Project Grant No. 4032–A66, Division of Chronic Diseases, Public Health Service, U. S. Department of Health, Education and Welfare, administered by the Philadelphia Health Research Fund. The cost of the first printing, April 1967, was paid from the Project Grant. The second printing, November 1967, was made possible through funds provided by the Philadelphia Health Research Fund. This edition was first published by Doubleday & Company, Inc., 1968.

Dolphin Edition: 1973

# Dedication

Without the common bond of interest in the vital area of smoking and health on the part of the City of Philadelphia Administration of Mayor James H. J. Tate and the agencies listed here, the initial efforts of the City and these agencies in the sponsorship of the Philadelphia Smoking Project, and their continued support of it, the original publication of this book would not have been possible.

In acknowledgment of their substantial contribution in seeking solutions to the health problems posed by cigarettes, and for their continued inspiration and encouragement, this book is respectfully dedicated.

William A. Allen
Gerhard Angermann
William A. Fackler

Albert Einstein Medical Center
Diocesan School of Philadelphia
Hahnemann Medical College
Health & Welfare Council, Philadelphia District
Heart Association of Southeastern Pennsylvania
Pennsylvania Tuberculosis & Health Society
Pharmacy Council on Cigarette Smoking
Philadelphia Chapter American Cancer Society
Philadelphia College of Pharmacy & Science
Philadelphia County Medical Society
Philadelphia County Osteopathic Association
Philadelphia Health Research Fund

Philadelphia-Montgomery Tuberculosis & Health Association
Philadelphia Pharmacy Health Council
Philadelphia Public Health Department
School District of Philadelphia
Temple University-School of Pharmacy

# Foreword

The clear-cut evidence that cigarette smoking is detrimental to health continues to mount. Over five thousand documented studies published in the last four years have served to confirm the serious health risks attributable to smoking as originally reported to the nation in the January 1964 Surgeon General's report. In addition, the more recent statement of Surgeon General William H. Stewart in March 1966 that cigarettes are responsible for an excess of twelve million chronic ailments in this country beyond the expected yearly figures for non-smokers should serve to dispel any remaining doubts about the cigarette—health relationship.

The official disclosures regarding the dangers of cigarette smoking have caused many current smokers to become unhappy with their habit to a point where they are ready to stop. Many individual citizens, physicians, teachers, and other health professionals, moreover, have become interested in organizing and conducting local anti-smoking action programs. *Learning to Live Without Cigarettes* has been written specifically to fulfill the needs of both groups. Section I affords the current smoker with an opportunity to rid himself of his dependence on cigarettes by offering specific suggestions on how to quit, along with the latest information and newest insights on the peculiarities of the cigarette habit.

Section II of this book provides the professional worker with specific anti-smoking program activities that can be utilized in various community settings. The book concludes with an easy to read question and answer section that offers specific information on the extent of the health hazards of cigarette use.

The staff of the Philadelphia Smoking Project has had much practical experience in helping people break the cigarette habit and in conducting community anti-smoking programs. It is hoped that this knowledge and accumulated experience in the comparatively new field of smoking and health will be of help to smokers who wish to quit and to professionals who wish to help others to quit or, ideally, not to begin smoking cigarettes.

> Norman R. Ingraham, M.D.
> Health Commissioner City of Philadelphia and Chairman Community Council on Smoking and Health

# Contents

# Section I
# How to Stop Smoking

## Chapter 1
## Sighting the Target

### UNLEARNING A HABIT

A pleasant, shy, middle-aged lady stopped at our smoking and health display booth at a recent Public Health conference and told us that she believed that she held the record for the number of times anybody had stopped smoking cigarettes. We asked her if she was acquainted with Mark Twain's claim of having stopped smoking a hundred times. She said yes, she'd heard about it, "but" she added, "Mark Twain was always exaggerating." It turned out that she was on her thirteenth try, had been "clean" this time for more than nine months, and felt that finally she "had it made." We congratulated her and wished her good luck. Thirteen is considered an unlucky number, and it would be interesting to know whether she had finally learned, not only how to stop, but also how to stay off. It was quite obvious that she had learned the former. It was even more evident that she was learning the hard way.

Learning the hard way means learning by trial and error. To learn this way is a waste of time and energy and offers the possible chance of discouragement. In the case of quitting cigarettes, trial and error results also in the multiplication of physical and mental discomfort.

Learning the easy way, on the other hand, means arming yourself with as much information as possible on the subject of breaking habits in general, and the cigarette habit in particular. This does not necessarily mean that the cigarette habit will be easy to lick. On the contrary, because it is an extremely difficult habit to break, it would seem sensible to take every advantage of the considerable knowl-

edge now available on this subject and to learn whatever
devices, physical and psychological, have been discovered
to ease the discomfort of adjusting to a life without cigarettes. In addition to a body of facts that the smoker
should have, this section of the book offers him a co-
ordinated program that will help him wage an effective
campaign in his war against his enemy—the cigarette.

If you are a long-term smoker, you may have learned
the habit so well that you can go through all the motions
of lighting up without thinking about it, having forgotten
that your last cigarette may still be burning half used on
your ash tray. It was, incidentally, just such a situation
that triggered President Eisenhower's determination to give
up the habit. The point is that a habit so well learned ob-
viously takes a bit of unlearning. For many smokers, the
cigarette habit was not easy to learn. They had to try many
times before they mastered it. Some, of course, never succeeded and finally gave up trying, in spite of all the help
that was available through the high-powered, seductive
appeals of the cigarette advertisements in TV, press, and
radio, not to mention the urging of friends.

The preceding remarks are intended to emphasize that
no quick or easy cure is possible for such a complex and
long ingrained habit. Any change in the modification of a
smoking habit, to be successful and permanent, must be
accompanied by changes in attitudes relating to it. A first
step, therefore, in the business of unlearning the cigarette
habit must be a willingness to listen to some new facts or
at least, to take a fresh look at old ones. You may already
be acquainted with some of the material you will find in
this book, but it will be well for you to assume that you
know nothing.

Let us illustrate. You may be thoroughly convinced that
smoking cigarettes is dangerous to your health. You feel,
therefore, that you can skip Section III, which describes
specifically the damages to body tissues that result in the
diseases associated with cigarette smoking. You now meet a
friend who asks you why you have stopped smoking. You
reply that you are convinced that cigarettes are bad for
your health. All exaggerated, he says, and you reply in

general terms of disease relationships and quote some appropriate statistics. He is unconvinced, as many smokers still are, and he may now, by his skepticism, cause you to doubt your own beliefs. If, on the other hand, you can tell him that some agent from his inhaled smoke paralyzes the cilia, the tiny hairlike structures that are found in the inner lining of the lungs, and, therefore, inhibits the filtering mechanism of the lungs, making the smoker vulnerable not only to the harmful effects of his own smoking, but, in addition, vulnerable to the cancer producing agents present in the polluted air that all of us must breathe, you now have not only cast doubts on his own belief and made a possible convert, but you have also done something very important for yourself. In the process of countering his arguments, you have helped to convince yourself of your position on smoking, and to that extent have reinforced your determination to be rid of the cigarette habit. Therein lies the importance of learning all you can about the subject of smoking as a costly, slavish, and dangerous practice. The more you know about it, the more you will become convinced of the logic and the rightness of your decision to quit. This, in turn, will provide you with the determination or motivation that is the most essential element in any program designed to break the cigarette habit.

In conclusion, then, you must be prepared to be active on your own behalf in your plans to learn how to live without cigarettes. You cannot expect to sit passively by and hope for a magic pill or formula to do the work for you. Without the facts that will change your thinking and attitudes about smoking, you can hardly expect to be successful in your battle to live without cigarettes.

# Chapter 2
## Your Enemy, the Cigarette

### WHAT MAKES YOU SMOKE?

A woman who will probably never get off cigarettes called on the telephone to ask when our clinic would be held. We gave her the information. "What do you do at the clinics?" she then asked. We started to explain our program of education coupled with group discussion. "You mean," she interrupted "you just talk?" We were mulling over what answer we could give to that question. We didn't want to discourage her unnecessarily by asking her in turn, "Do you know a better way?" when she interrupted our train of thought to say, "I don't think I'd be interested in that. I thought maybe I could get hypnotized, or you could give me a pill."

She hung up, just as a good answer to her original question came to us. The next time someone asks us whether we just talk at the smokers' clinics, we will say, "Yes, we do talk, and we also listen."

Experience with thousands of smokers whom we have questioned about their smoking habits and attitudes shows that only a very small number have found reasons for stopping that are compelling enough for them to become successful ex-smokers. Many have confessed that they have come to the clinic in hopes of being persuaded to stop. Others, who think they ought to quit, believe that the clinic is an easy solution to their problem. The trick of a successful clinic is to hold both kinds long enough to get them to understand that the help they will need to break the cigarette habit must eventually come from within.

If the reader is currently smoking, it is apparent that

he has not found compelling enough reasons for stopping, or he would not now be reading this book. He may find his compelling reasons in this chapter, or in the next, or the one after that. Others have found them in this book, and have licked their habit. However, since reasons, or needs, for smoking differ for each individual, reasons to stop must necessarily differ, and the reader must continue to search for those reasons that fit his particular case. Finally, he must be ready to apply those countermeasures appropriate to his individual smoking problem that will help him to achieve first control, and then mastery, over his habit.

The smoking habit is an overlapping and interrelated complex that reflects a variety of emotional needs, conscious and unconscious, real or imaginary, that vary not only from smoker to smoker, but also from cigarette to cigarette. For example, a smoker may feel the need for a cigarette to help him through a critical conference during working hours, and then smoke later in the evening to relax after dinner.

It becomes obvious that if the smoker cannot find the reason or combination of reasons for giving up cigarettes that are at least as strong as those which compel him to continue smoking, he will hardly succeed in quitting. His first task, then, should be to try to understand why he smokes. Behaviorial scientists who have been studying the problem distinguish between two principal types of smoking behavior. The first is defined as smoking for the purpose of increasing positive affect. (Affect as used here designates feeling, as in affection.) It presumably means that the smoker is smoking to increase a feeling of well-being, either through the stimulative or the relaxing effects of tobacco. The second type of smoking behavior is defined as smoking for the purpose of decreasing negative affect, that is, to diminish the depressive effects in individuals brought on by such factors as anxiety, frustration, or boredom. A third type of smoking behavior is also distinguished, namely, that of the habituated smoker, who smokes automatically, from sheer habit, without reference to the specific needs that would be satisfied in the other two types of smoking behavior.

Except for the habituated smoker, then, a person smokes to get a measure of relief from tensions that may be precipitated by a wide variety of situations. If he is alone or at work, a cigarette will relieve tensions that result from anger, fear, boredom, or frustration. He may smoke also to relieve tensions resulting from the excitement of good news, the elation over a successful business deal, the prospect of a promotion or salary increase, or the promise of an adventure with a new acquaintance.

If, on the other hand, the smoker is not alone, but in a group (many people smoke only in social settings, as at banquets, cocktail parties, bowling, or card games), he may be smoking for different reasons. He may smoke in response to the exhilaration of good fellowship, to a desire to be one of the group (or at least not to appear as an outsider), to be considered debonair or sophisticated, or to get the comfort of having something to do with his hands.

To sum up, his smoking, whether alone or in a crowd, fulfills a variety of needs, the fulfillment of which constitutes a pleasant experience. The needs, by the way, may be real or imaginary, but that makes no difference. They are there, and *if they are not satisfied by a cigarette, the smoker will find himself in various degrees of discomfort.* This rarely happens, because cigarettes are almost always available. Cigarette smokers are notoriously generous in offering help to those who have momentarily run short. Every cigarette smoker is careful before he leaves for work, or a party, to make sure that he has a sufficient supply for the day or evening, as the case may be, with a few to spare.

We have emphasized the sentence in the preceding paragraph because it is a critical one. It holds the key to the understanding of the physiological and psychological aspects of cigarette addiction. It answers the question posed in the subtitle "What Makes You Smoke?" by helping the would-be ex-smoker to understand the mechanism whereby cigarette smoke can produce such apparently benign effects as stimulation and relaxation, even though these effects seem to be contradictory. It reveals at the same time the mechanism of internal injury from cigarette smoke, disclosing to him the heavy price that he must pay for the satisfactions he believes he is getting from his habit.

Of course, some smokers couldn't care less about how the agreeable sensations of smoking are produced, or how and to what extent the damage to bodily organs occurs. But the man who would win a victory over such a worthy, wily, opponent as the cigarette habit had better learn what he can about the practice beforehand, so that he can at least give his opponent a respectable fight when they tangle.

It was believed for many years that the nicotine in the tobacco was responsible for the pleasing effects of smoking, and that the tars in the inhaled smoke were responsible for the injurious effects. Such a view is still essentially correct, except that a number of modifications of this somewhat oversimplified statement are necessary in the light of more recent scientific findings.

It is true that nicotine is responsible for the pleasing effects of smoking, but not because it is a beneficial substance. Nicotine is deadly poison, a single drop of which injected into the blood stream can kill an adult. As such, it has a number of injurious effects on the human organism, to say nothing of its habit-forming propensities. But the pleasing effects or "lift" that is produced by nicotine are only the side effects of the body's defense mechanism trying to rid itself of the poison.

As is well known, the human body has built-in protective mechanisms that move into action whenever the wellbeing of the individual is threatened. You may be sure that when you see the hair rising on the back of an animal that is threatened by danger, that its heart is also pounding to circulate the blood through its system to mobilize all its defensive powers.

When nicotine enters the blood stream, the heartbeat immediately accelerates, in some individuals up to 40 per cent. This results in an increased blood flow, which can be measured by a rise in blood pressure. The increased flow of blood through the system speeds up the chemical processes of the body. More oxygen is delivered to the brain, and more energy is furnished to the body cells and organs. This energy, in the form of fuel sugars, has been in the liver as a result of the simultaneous secretion of adrenalin into the blood stream. These fuel sugars, when burned by oxygen in the body's cells, produce energy which normally is needed to live and work. In the smoker, though, they are needed to break down the toxic elements of the nicotine, so that they can be quickly eliminated through the kidneys. The increased heartbeat helps to hasten the process.

It is this increase in the flow of blood as a result of the body's reaction to nicotine that also results in the feeling of stimulation or "lift" that is experienced by the smoker when he inhales nicotine. And it is this feeling of well-being that helps the smoker to rise momentarily above the tensions or frustrations, or the problems of his daily existence. If the nicotine in the tobacco and the tar in the smoke were not so injurious to the human organism, how pleasant it would be for all of us to sit back and smoke our troubles away!

Incidentally, the feeling of relaxation that smokers claim as one of the effects of smoking is nothing more than a reaction of the human organism to the initial stimulation brought about by nicotine. As the effects of the nicotine wear off, the heartbeat returns to normal, and the body processes slow down. The presence of carbon monoxide in the smoke may account for some of the sedative effects, but artificial stimulation of the nervous system always results in the deceleration of the spirit, inducing quiescence, languor, and finally depression.

We spoke earlier of the feelings of discomfort that arise when the smoker cannot satisfy his need for a smoke, either because of the unavailability of cigarettes, or a smoking prohibition, and the importance of this fact as a clue to an understanding of the nature of the cigarette habit. The need, or urge, to smoke is a demand by the body for the fuel sugars mentioned earlier. This demand is triggered by the autonomic nervous system when the fuel sugars have been momentarily depleted from the blood stream. Blood sugar deficiency manifests itself in feelings of fatigue and depression. The regular smoker has accustomed his nervous system to expect a regular artificial injection of the powerful drug—nicotine—that prods the blood pumping apparatus into action. When the expected stimulation for some reason is not forthcoming, a depressing effect, which has been aptly called "smokers' tension" results. This nervous malaise can be relieved only by more nicotine in the form of a cigarette. In other words, the smoker has become slave to a habit, which in effect says, "Either you will now smoke, or I shall make you feel miserable until you do."

We shall not be surprised if the average smoker does not accept this view of his smoking habit. Many smokers do not care to see themselves in the image of tobacco slaves. They simply deny the existence of such a possibility even though a twenty-four-hour abstinence from smoking would convince them soon enough. The human psyche has also defense mechanisms for filtering out unpleasant and unpalatable facts. The smoker who wants to find excuses for continuing to smoke can find them in abundance. If the following are not on his list, he may feel free to use them.

1. There is only a statistical association between smoking and lung cancer, heart disease, and respiratory diseases, so how can you blame these ailments on cigarettes?

2. The exact cause of cancer has not been found.

3. Not all doctors agree that smoking causes all those diseases.

4. Many smokers live a long time.

5. You have to die from something sometime.

6. Smoking is better than being a nervous wreck, or using tranquilizers, or drinking to excess.

7. All those sixty million smokers can't be wrong.

8. Life is full of all kinds of hazards, so why not enjoy yourself smoking?

9. Smoking is better than putting on a lot of weight.

10. The increased incidence of lung cancer does not reflect an increase in cigarette consumption. It can be accounted for by improved diagnostic techniques.

One of the smoker's favorite excuses, alas, he can no longer use, namely: "If cigarettes are as bad as they are alleged to be, the government would require a warning label on the package as it does on other dangerous products."

If we thought we could convince a single smoker of the fallacies of these statements, we would take the time to refute them. But we must get on.

There are three stages in the evolution of the smoking habit. The initial stage combines the experimental, where curiosity first and the desire for peer and adult status later are the chief elements. The second stage is characterized by the development of a physical dependence on nicotine stimulation, the mechanics of which have just been described at length. The third stage, involving the psychological dependence of the individual upon the smoking ritual, will now be discussed.

It can be easily demonstrated that in this third stage, the smoker's use of cigarettes goes beyond the specific needs for which he smoked formerly, and that the satisfaction he now derives from smoking are for the most part psychological in nature.

In exploring this idea, the smoker may well discover that he has been kidding himself about his smoking needs. Let us consider the need that many smokers seem to feel for a cigarette to help them over a crisis. We will use the term "crisis" here to cover any tension-producing situation, good or bad. It would now seem that a pack-a-day smoker experiences about twenty crises each day, and a two pack-a-day smoker about forty crises. It seems strange that these crises recur with such a degree of regularity for these smokers. We do not say it is an impossible phenomenon, for certain jobs make specific and perhaps routine demands on people. But we have all observed that the same smokers who smoke the same daily quota of cigarettes on the job, smoke the same number of cigarettes when they are off the job, evenings out, weekends, or on extended vacations.

One of the writers of this book was a teacher for many years. Teaching can be hard work, loaded with tension-charged situations. This writer firmly believed, and repeatedly stated, that the only thing that helped him to get through the day was the friendly, between-class cigarette that gave him the needed lift to survive the next forty-five minute bout with a class of spirited teen-agers. It had never occurred to him that during his vacations in Canada, while basking in the summer sun, fishing, and relaxing, he continued to smoke his daily quota of cigarettes without reference to those situations on the job that clearly seemed to justify his smoking. Indeed, he always made sure to supply himself in advance with ten cartons of his favorite brand to carry him over the summer.

When the writer quit after twenty-five years of smoking, he realized that he had been kidding himself for years about his need for cigarettes. He continued to teach for five years longer, and amused himself watching his smoking associates puffing away frantically between classes, kidding themselves as he had done, that cigarettes were indispensable to their survival on the job.

The obvious conclusion of the foregoing, if it needs spelling out, is that the smoker becomes habituated to the need for cigarettes *in accordance with his daily quota*, without regard to situations involving stress. This point is emphasized because many smokers refuse to admit that their smoking has become a habit independent of the usual smoking-triggered situations, personal or social, which they believe necessitates their continued smoking.

It makes little difference to the average smoker whether his needs for a cigarette are real or imaginary, that is, physical or psychological. They are there, as we said before, and if they are not satisfied, discomfort will follow. However, it is important for the smoker who is trying to terminate his dependence on cigarettes to distinguish between the real needs and the psychological, so that he can apply those countermeasures that are appropriate to either or both of these elements of the cigarette habit.

Another important fact the would-be ex-smoker should also know is the price he is paying for the pleasant sensations that are occasioned by the nicotine from his cigarette. We have described those pleasures and the mechanics whereby they arise. Before we describe the harmful effects that result from tobacco use, it might be well to take a last look at the "pleasures" for what they really are, so that the smoker may be in a good position to balance the pleasures of smoking against their cost.

Many smokers honestly believe they enjoy smoking, in

spite of a survey by the American Cancer Society which showed that only 16 per cent admitted to finding smoking pleasurable. As stated earlier, the "pleasure" of smoking cigarettes lies in the gratification either of the smoker's self-induced craving for nicotine or a related psychological compulsion. It is not a positive pleasure, in the sense of a delight or a joy, but a negative one, comparable to the relief one gets when an injection of Novocain deadens the pain of an aching tooth. In simple language, the regular smoker smokes to avoid the discomfort of not smoking. And if he thinks cigarettes are an absolute necessity, what about the fifty million non-smoking adult Americans who, man for man, occupation for occupation, get through the average working day of tension, frustrations, worries, and boredom happily and efficiently, without having to call on the help of a cigarette twenty, thirty, or forty times a day. Who is kidding whom?

Let us listen now for a moment as J. D. Lewis, founder of Nicotine Unlimited, permits YOUR ENEMY, THE CIGARETTE, to speak: "Go ahead, sucker, stick me in your mouth and light me up. I'm poison, and although it might take me a little longer, I can eventually do as much damage to your insides as a dumdum bullet. I cause jumping nerves in men and women. I can impart momentary poise to the embarrassed, a measure of courage to the timid, and give some false solace to those who have encountered mental discomfort. Because of these temporary stimulations, I am tolerated despite knowledge of my capacity to do harm. I am subtle, for unannounced to the user, I trap him. I conquer his will power. He becomes slowly but surely an addict. I make him my slave."

It is an eloquent description of perhaps the principal indictment of nicotine. Its addictive properties make it responsible for the perpetuation not only of its own special injurious effects, but also for the development of all the other diseases, such as lung cancer, chronic bronchitis, and emphysema that result from the addictive inhalation of the many tar compounds present in cigarette smoke.

Nicotine itself is harmful in its constricting effect on the blood vessels. This constrictive effect has been explained as another defense mechanism to minimize the spread of the nicotine through the system. Its effect on the closing off of the capillaries in the hands and feet can be readily demonstrated by comparing the surface temperature of the hands or feet before and during a smoke. Some smokers contract Buerger's disease, which is characterized by an impairment of the circulation in hands and feet. The reduced nutrition and oxygen supply leads to gangrene, and often amputation of feet and legs result when such smokers persist in their smoking.

In addition, a number of studies have indicated that nicotine is responsible for the release of larger amounts of cholesterol into the blood stream. Furthermore, the retention in the bladder of the toxic elements of nicotine awaiting elimination accounts for the much higher rates of cancer of the bladder among smokers as compared to non-smokers. Finally, the premature aging processes involved in the constant metabolic speed-up caused by the repeated stimulation of nicotine results in the now well-established fact of reduced life expectancy among cigarette smokers.

The cigarette, of course, is the smoker's enemy in more ways than one. Even though the smoker is willing to gamble, and play Russian roulette with his health, he may not be willing to pay all the additional blackmail that his habit is extracting from him for the privilege of smoking. We invite him, therefore, to turn to Chapter 3 to consider further the exorbitant costs of his habit.

# Chapter 3
## Smoke Now—Pay Later

### THE HIGH COSTS OF SMOKING

In the previous chapters, we explained that the smoker must have a good reason to stop smoking or he will never make it. Many smokers have thought seriously about the idea of giving up cigarettes, but their determination has not yet "firmed" to the point where they are ready to commit all their mental, physical, and moral resources to the effort. Where the smoker is not yet ready for the effort, he might better wait until he is. When a firm resolution has been reached to be finished with the cigarette habit for good, there is no problem about quitting. No one can convert a smoker's wishes or desires into a firm resolve except the smoker himself. A sensible approach for any smoker who is trying to find arguments to enforce his decision to stop smoking is to take a good look at the possible consequences of his continued smoking.

First of all, if the smoking of cigarettes were not so dangerous to health, the other drawbacks discussed here might be at least tolerable, although many former smokers have found them serious enough to give up the habit regardless of the health dangers. What makes the cigarette habit so dangerous, as compared with habits like excessive drinking or driving at excessive speeds, is that the bad effects are not immediately noticeable. Some smokers can smoke for years without ill effects, or shall we say noticeable ill effects, simply because the ill effects are cumulative. Suddenly, without warning, a heart attack occurs or a lung cancer develops. Certain disabilities, such as shortness of breath, smoker's cough, or a peptic ulcer, may appear earlier. Crippling diseases, like chronic bronchitis, emphysema, and Buerger's disease, appear somewhat later. The killer diseases, like heart disease and lung cancer, may not appear for twenty or thirty years, but they strike quite suddenly and without warning.

If the future seems far away for the smoker, and he feels, therefore, that he will have plenty of time to think about quitting, let him listen to Dr. Linus Pauling, internationally famous scientist, and twice a Nobel prize winner, who says, "A one-pack-a-day smoker at the age of fifty is as old physiologically as a non-smoker aged fifty-eight. A two-pack-a-day smoker at fifty is as old as a non-smoker aged sixty-six, and a smoker who has smoked three packs a day all his life, at age fifty is as old physiologically and has the same high incidence of disease as the average non-smoker at age seventy-four." Now, the smoker who puts off quitting cigarettes until he is fifty, according to Dr. Pauling, won't be fifty. Agewise, he will be fifty-eight, or if he has smoked two packs of cigarettes every day, he will be sixty-six! Dr. Pauling has calculated further that each cigarette smoked cuts down life expectancy by 14.4 minutes. Every time a smoker has finished a cigarette he has shortened his life span about a quarter of an hour.

So you see, no smoker can escape the evil consequences of his habit, even if he is fortunate enough to avoid a heart attack or a lung cancer. Premature aging is the certain fate of the cigarette addict. Even the unborn children of smoking mothers are innocent victims of this all-encompassing evil. Miscarriage, premature birth, and underweight babies have resulted from smoking by mothers during pregnancy.

The complete story of the disease-producing capabilities of the cigarette has not yet been written. For those who are interested in learning what is known to date of the evil effects of cigarettes, we have reserved a separate section at the end of the book which describes the principal ailments resulting from cigarette use together with the extensive supporting evidence. The report of the Surgeon General's advisory committee is the source of this information. Complete details may be had from the original report.

If the smoker is not concerned about his health, now or in the future, there are other costs that can be charged to the smoking habit.

Let him consider the cost of smoking, for instance:

1. In the price he is paying, moneywise, for his smoking. Couples who have quit smoking and kept records have reported savings of $400 a year. In England, where cigarettes now cost $.75 a pack (New York State now $.50), a steady smoker at the retirement age of sixty-two would have spent the equivalent of $10,000 for his smoking. Add to this the potential interest, and you have an even larger amount. Imagine having more than $10,000 in the bank as a nest egg at retirement.

Let the smoker consider the cost of smoking, also . . .

2. Moneywise, for expenses related to prolonged illnesses and disability. Smokers spend twice as much time in hospitals as do non-smokers. Doctors have to be paid, there are losses in income for sick leave, and hospital fees are spiraling.

Let the smoker who may be the parent of young children consider the cost of smoking, also . . .

3. In the loss of the respect of his children, who have a right to look to him for guidance in the matter of their health. The smoking parent can tell his children that smoking is dangerous to their health, but when the children see the parent continue to smoke, what are they to think? The preachment of "Do as I say, not as I do," has never been a good basis for the moral instruction of youth. Young children are confused by it, and older children sense the hypocrisy of it. The resulting loss of confidence and faith in the parent by his children, and the doubts that may arise with regard to other child-parent relationships, is one of the costs that the smoking parent must add to the rest of his liabilities.

Let the smoker, parent or not, consider the cost of smoking, also . . .

4. In the loss of his self-respect, in that he finds himself dictated to by a three-inch cylinder of shredded tobacco leaf. It is strange that in this country, where we pride ourselves so much on our determination not to let ourselves be pushed around, we submit so meekly to the dictates of nicotine. Having said that, we are happy to report that just as many smokers have quit the cigarette habit to achieve independence from tobacco slavery as have quit for reasons of health.

This might be a good place to discuss one of the more subtle evils of the cigarette habit that is listed only rarely in the already extensive catalogue of miseries laid to cigarettes. It is perhaps here that the reader may finally discover the reason sufficient and adequate enough to divorce himself from the cigarette habit.

Countless thousands of smokers have permitted cigarettes to dominate their lives. Their daily existence has become so cigarette centered that all their waking activities are regulated by their smoking habit: a cigarette on awakening, one before breakfast, one with coffee, one after coffee, one waiting for the subway, one getting out of the subway, etc., etc., etc. It is a daily ritual strictly adhered to without deviation. No wonder the housewife, off cigarettes for two weeks and nervous as a cat, answered, when asked the time of day by her husband, "It's two cigarettes after eight."

The loss of taste and smell are minor casualties compared to the loss of all those moments that were formerly devoted to other creative pursuits that brought so much rich variety to living, when a person's capacity to enjoy the pleasures of the life about him did not require the artificial stimulation of an adrenalin prod; nor did the quiet, restful moments of life need to be artificially induced by pill or cigarette. The confirmed smoker has lost much of his capacity for the simplest pleasures of life because he has accustomed his brain and nervous system to a daily succession of high-level nicotine jolts.

No wonder he is satisfied just to sit and smoke. To get any pleasure from one's own creativity is too much time and trouble. Why use up one's energy when a cigarette fills the need or the void? To use a line from the popular song, which might well be called the cigarette smoker's creed:

> No more will I go 'round this world
> For I have found my world in you.

If the reader has higher aspirations for his life and is not satisfied with the foregoing image of himself as a smoker, now or in the future, he may be ready to consider what steps he may take to avoid the prospects of so dismal a future.

To sum up, the costs of smoking add up to a staggering total. What is there on the credit side of the ledger to balance so formidable a debit? Upon close examination, there can't possibly be that much pleasure in smoking, especially when that pleasure is as dubious, negative, and illusory as we have described it earlier.

# Chapter 4
## Combat Ready

### THE WISH VS. THE WANT TO STOP

At a meeting of a smoking withdrawal clinic, the speaker, a psychiatrist, had asked for five volunteers to assist him in a demonstration of group psychotherapy. Seventy other clinic participants moved up close to listen. "I want you all to tell me," he began, "why you enrolled in this clinic. Who will begin?"

It was clear from the general hesitation that none of the five panelists had formulated any precise reason or set of reasons for their decision to try to give up cigarettes. Finally, a young, attractive girl in the group spoke up. "I've stopped smoking several times during the past year, but I've always started back again. I thought maybe I could learn how to stop smoking permanently." "Excuse me," said the doctor, "what we want to know is, why do you want to give up smoking?" "Oh," answered the young lady, "I don't know, I guess it's because I'm terrified of death, have always been, I don't know why. And if cigarettes shorten your life . . . you see, I have two little girls, and I want to see them grow up and have babies, and I want to see what they'd be like and enjoy them." She looked around at the group as much as to say she hoped she had not said anything too embarrassing. The psychiatrist nodded his head as he considered her case. "That's a good reason for giving up cigarettes," he said, "even if it is a selfish one." The young mother was startled at first by this unexpected response, then puzzled, as was the listening audience. "Have you ever considered how your children would feel," he asked her, "if you were taken ill?" He turned to the whole group. "I wonder how many parents have ever stopped to think how distressed children can be even at the thought of parental illness, let alone the possibility of fatal illness."

Everybody got the point. It couldn't have been more obvious. The young lady had been thinking only in terms of her own loss and deprivation, should she fall victim to any cigarette induced illness. And so had all the rest. In two minutes the assembled group had realized another reason for giving up smoking: that those who depend on them for livelihood and affection, and who have a stake in their welfare, are deserving of consideration in this matter of health risk.

Another lady on the panel confessed, as her reason for wishing to give up cigarettes, that she had been ill with chronic bronchitis for eight years. The doctor pursed his lips as he considered her case. "It is quite obvious that you are a very brave lady," he said, slowly, "but it is also obvious that you do not want to stop smoking."

The lady looked at the doctor incredulously, as though she had not heard properly. Again the audience exchanged looks of puzzlement. "As a matter of fact," continued the doctor, slowly, addressing himself now to the whole assembly, "not one of you who is enrolled in this clinic really wants to stop smoking. Otherwise—" he waited for the effects of this surprising statement to subside—"Otherwise," he repeated, "none of you would be here now. You would have stopped smoking long ago."

We shall not try to describe the effect of this statement on the assembled group. A dozen hands were raised simultaneously in challenge. Not everybody was ready to accept the doctor's word. He, in turn, shrugged his shoulders and said, "But I am a reasonable man. If you want to argue with me I will listen, although I can not understand how you can argue a point of such unassailable logic. When you tell me why you think you would like to stop smoking, I will tell you what your words are actually saying to me."

Then, for the next hour, he gave an extraordinarily moving demonstration of how a talented, skillful psychiatrist can reveal to a group of people the inner conflict of opposing forces in the human psyche that prevents individuals from achieving those goals that they desperately want to achieve. "Only," he concluded, "as the desires of the conscious mind coincide with, or support, the desire of the subconscious mind, will an individual be successful in solving his problems, whether the problem be overweight, alcohol, or tobacco. Half of you are here tonight because you want to shift to someone else the responsibility for your indulging in a habit that you are unhappy with. The other half are here because you want to be persuaded that you should stop smoking. All of you still have some unconscious reservations, a reluctance to make a complete break with a habit that your reason tells you is expensive, slavish, and dangerous. Until your inner being, your subconscious mind, is similarly convinced, you will not be successful. As long as you entertain the idea that smoking is *attractive* in any way, and that giving it up involves any sacrifice, you will continue to be the victim of that inner conflict that prevents you from giving up the habit. Until you can learn to hate this habit to which you are now a slave, for all the misery it can bring to you, your friends, and your fellow man, now and in the future, you will continue to be miserable with your habit. I can only hope you will be persuaded by what you see and hear at these meetings and discussions, to the point where your subconscious mind will be convinced, that cigarettes are definitely out as far as you are concerned. At that point, you will have no difficulty in putting cigarettes out of your life."

The question now arises, how does one go about convincing the subconscious of the desirability of giving up a bad habit? Our doctor gave a good illustration of it in the course of his "therapy." The lady with chronic bronchitis was on the verge of tears with frustration as she tried to convince him that she really wanted to give up smoking. "Honestly, I do want to give up smoking. I hate it. It is ruining my life." The doctor pretended that he had not heard. "Would you mind repeating what you have just said. I don't believe I heard every word. It is really important, and I want to hear you say it again." The lady repeated it, this time more emphatically and with a trace of irritation at not being believed. "I'm sorry," said the doctor, "but you still have not convinced me. But I don't want you to be angry with me. Maybe you have convinced some of these others. Has she convinced you?" he asked, turning to a young man on the panel, who had expressed amazement earlier that anyone with a long-standing case of chronic bronchitis could continue to smoke. "Tell him what you have just told me," he asked her. The lady repeated her statement now for the third time. The young man hesitated to embarrass her by expressing an opinion. Finally, the doctor got the lady to repeat her statement for the whole group. Then he said to her, "Now, I don't know whether you have convinced anybody present, but I'm sure if you can keep repeating this statement to yourself often enough, you might convince yourself that you mean what you are saying."

The psychiatrist was demonstrating, of course, the age-old psychological principle of convincing oneself of a belief by constant repetition. The principle of repetition, as everyone knows, is basic to the merchandising of consumer goods, and if, as in the case of cigarettes, the smoker has been hypnotized by the constant repetition that they can do something for him, he must reverse the process and convince himself that he is much better off without them.

Most psychologists who have been experimenting with the problem of cigarette addiction would agree today that the hypnotic effect of repeated suggestion is more effective in smoking deterrence than the posthypnotic suggestion offered to the subject under hypnotic trance.

A number of interesting experiments are being conducted to develop techniques for reaching the subconscious mind and in using its powerful effect in creating aversion to cigarette smoking. One psychologist tried to help his wife off cigarettes by arranging for her to get a mild electric shock whenever she helped herself to a cigarette from a special container. It was his theory that, even though she might develop a tolerance for the shock, in time a subconscious dislike for cigarettes would develop.

Another psychologist experimented with the technique of entirely bypassing the conscious mind in his effort to build up, without the knowledge of the smoking subject, an aversion to the cigarette habit. He developed an ingenious device, triggered by an infrared light, that introduced unpleasant noise into the tape recording of a favorite musical score whenever the smoking subject took a puff on his cigarette. It is a promising field for experimentation.

There is the story of the famous movie actor who attributes his success over the cigarette habit to a devoted wife who, over a period of several months, convinced him in soft whispers, while he was sleeping, that smoking was a bad habit.

Until an easy and foolproof remedy for cigarette addiction is found, however, the smoker who wants to be free of his habit now must rely on whatever resources are available at the moment. These are considerable, and it may be appropriate at this point to review what they are and how they may be most effectively utilized.

Earlier in the book we made the statement that many smokers fail in their attempts to give up cigarettes because they are not ready to commit all of their mental, physical, and moral resources to the struggle. Chapter 2 acquainted the reader with the nature of the cigarette habit and its adverse effects on health Chapter 3 revealed the exorbitant costs of the cigarette habit. This chapter should have provided the reader with sufficient and adequate reasons, if he needed them, to support a genuine determination to kick his habit once and for all. In the present chapter the authors have tried to give the reader some insight into the psychological conflicts that may hamper the smoker's success in breaking the habit. The succeeding chapters will reveal the stratagems that are useful in cutting the cigarette habit down to size, that is, into manageable bits, setting realistic and attainable goals with useful hints on how to minimize the discomforts of the withdrawal process.

All of this knowledge is power, and the smoker who uses it intelligently has a much better chance of success than the smoker who tries to give up the habit without these aids. Still, knowledge alone cannot guarantee success. There are other resources that the smoker must bring into play to help him when the urge to resume smoking plagues him, as it surely will from time to time.

We very often credit the successful ex-smoker with being a person of strong will, without considering that will power is simply the outer manifestation of inner strength based on moral principle. The young lad bears his pain in silence because he believes it is unmanly to shed tears. A smoker wills himself to give up his habit because he cannot reconcile his slavery to the habit with his belief in the duty of a man to be the master of his actions. A parent will give up the smoking habit, or any other bad habit, in the belief that it is his duty to set an example of good living for his young children. The Seventh-day Adventist will not use tobacco because he regards his body as the temple of his Creator, and that it is his duty to preserve such a priceless gift from all injurious influences.

In the many five-day smokers' clinics that the Seventh-day Adventists have organized throughout the country to persuade and assist others in giving up the smoking habit, prayer is recommended for those who need help in resisting the temptation to smoke. If the reader thinks, with others, that prayer has gone out of fashion, he will surely not deny its psychological effectiveness, and he certainly cannot quarrel with its success in producing countless thousands of converts in the five-day clinics of this religious order.

The point is that the smoker who wants to give himself every chance to be successful must be ready to use all the resources he can muster, and if prayer is one of them, so much the better. As we conclude this chapter, let the reader now take stock of his resources and reflect whether, with the aid he has received thus far in his reading and with the help he can glean from the remaining chapters, he believes he can make a real fight of it!

# Chapter 5
## Battle Strategy

### OUTWITTING THE ENEMY

A large and complex problem is best solved by breaking it down into smaller units and tackling these units one at a time. Breaking a cigarette habit, which certainly qualifies as a complex and stubborn problem, must be handled in the same way.

First of all, the nature of the habit must be studied; second, the remedies or tactics that have helped successful ex-smokers must be understood; and third, those remedies that meet the specific needs of a particular smoking problem must be intelligently applied.

The cigarette exerts two holds on the smoker, one being physiological (physical), the other psychological. The first results from the pharmacological (chemical or biological) effects of nicotine on the brain and the nervous system. When the body has been accustomed to the regular stimulating effects of nicotine (we could call it emotional fuel), which we have described previously, a sudden withholding or deprivation of the expected nicotine results in varying degrees of discomfort. This distress, commonly referred to as withdrawal symptoms, differs both in degree and duration among smokers of quite similar smoking habits, because individuals differ widely both in their sensitivity to the effects of nicotine and in their toleration of pain. The symptoms range from feelings of disorientation, restlessness, nervousness, agitation, anxiety, to panic. A traffic policeman whose relief turned up fifteen minutes late was overheard to say, "I can't talk to you now, Joe. If I don't get a cigarette right away, I'll have a nicotine fit."

One wonders what agony, in the way of withdrawal distress, would await a person with so strong a dependence upon cigarettes, were he to try to quit. Yet it is not the strength of one's addiction that determines the severity of withdrawal distress. The key factor is motivation. Those smokers with strong motivation to quit generally experience very mild, almost negligible distress.

Many ex-smokers have admitted that their actual discomfort, looking back, was not much more severe than one would experience during the course of a common cold. We take the discomfort of a cold in stride because we know the outside limits of that discomfort in degree and duration. If someone could say to a smoker that he will be free from withdrawal distress in three days or a week, or even ten days, he would not mind tolerating that distress as long as he could be certain of a definite time limit.

Unfortunately, no one can give a smoker any such assurance. In addition to the physical discomforts, very often magnified into bizarre aberrations, there are also psychological ties between the smoker and his habit that complicate the quitting procedure, which results frequently in a prolongation of the withdrawal distress. Psychological dependence on the cigarette habit lasts for a much longer period and may, if the smoker is not on his guard, result in a relapse even after an abstinence of six months or longer.

The *psychological* addiction of cigarette smoking covers the whole complex of activities associated with smoking: (1) those related to individual smoking triggered situations involving personal anxieties, frustrations, or boredom, and (2) social smoking at such affairs as coffee breaks, cocktail parties, card games, and spectator sports. In these situations, the impulse to resume smoking may be characterized not as a *craving* for a cigarette, but rather as a longing for one. It is not a physical pain or discomfort, but rather an emotional pang. We are not just playing with words. There is a real distinction involved. The would-be ex-smoker's memory is recalling subconsciously all those pleasure-filled experiences of the past that have been associated in his mind with cigarette smoking. He is making the common error of assuming that it was the cigarette and not the fellowship at the parties, the dances, the sleigh rides, or the stroll through the woods in the springtime that gave the pleasure.

It has been one of the triumphs of Madison Avenue to have deluded a whole generation of smokers into believing that the cigarette has been responsible for the pleasure they experience when they are skiing on snow or water, or swimming, or sailing, or roller coasting, or just sun bathing on the beach. It is only natural, therefore, for the ex-smoker to experience a desire for a cigarette, from time to time, long after the physical craving for the stimulating effects of nicotine has subsided. He has smoked for many years at happy occasions, and at a moment of low spirits may feel, after having decided to give up cigarettes, that all the fun and pleasure of the past is forever lost to him. People who have never smoked experience similar pangs and longings at the thought of pleasures that regretfully cannot be relived. They seem to survive.

Unless the smoker recognizes this impulse for what it really is, a snare and a delusion, he may foolishly succumb to the temptation to smoke. In a single moment he will be trapped again as a regular member of the great smoking society who, in their daily purchases of cigarettes, are making regular down payments on one or more future disabling illnesses, with resulting premature, unnecessary fatalities.

There are several other strange aspects of the cigarette habit that the smoker should be familiar with, besides its reluctance to permit a single smoker off the hook without exacting an exorbitant price. It is interesting to note that a smoking habit may not obey the smoker's wish not to smoke, but will obey a "No Smoking" sign, with very little discomfort to him. His habit will accept outside restrictions on its freedom quite willingly, such as fire regulations against smoking in public buildings, smoking on buses or subways, or smoking in the movie theaters. It will accept restrictions by parents who have laid down the no-smoking law. Although parental restrictions may be only limited restraints, they have been known to last for many years. Also, the smoking habit will accept restrictions imposed by the smoker himself, such as when he is lying down, or when he is sleeping. Many smokers regularly give up smoking once a year for forty days during Lent.

The point of all this is that the smoking habit is amenable to control. If it will obey restrictions imposed from without, it certainly can be brought under control from within. At the least, the would-be ex-smoker can profit from this knowledge by arranging to spend most of the first difficult twenty-four hours of stopping in situations where normally his habit has accepted restraints with little or no discomfort. A double feature movie can kill up to four hours of "waiting time."

One more aspect of the cigarette habit is worth mentioning. The regular smoker is "hooked" double; first on cigarettes, and second, on a brand. The advertisements tell the smoker that Bents, or Pluckies, or Big Deals—you name the brand—satisfy. Bents satisfy, they say, but they don't say what they satisfy. The smoker knows, however. He knows that Bents satisfy his need for a Bent cigarette—not for a Plucky, but for a Bent. When you desperately need a Bent, but none is available, a Plucky may do in an emergency.

Perhaps you remember the weekend away from home, when by some mistake you had to smoke a whole pack of those awful Pluckies rather than those good Bents. Of course, the other guy that got your brand by mistake had to smoke those foul Bents, rather than those great Pluckies. That's why smokers would rather fight than switch. As we said before, the smoker is hooked double; first, on cigarettes and second, on a brand.

One of the pioneers in smokers' withdrawal systems advised his smokers to switch brands every week for three weeks prior to Q-Day (quitting day). Switching brands is a good way to make smokers unhappy about their smoking, and the more dissatisfied a smoker is about smoking, the easier it will be for him to be rid of it.

In recent years, many smokers who are concerned about the health hazards of smoking have been switching to filter brand cigarettes, in the belief that the filter affords some protection. Published reports have shown, however, that some filter brands permit more tar and nicotine to pass than do non-filter brands. Now that tar and nicotine contents of all popular brands are available to smokers as a result of the Federal Trade Commission's testing program (see Table I page 30, more switching of brands may be expected, as a result of the smoker's search for "safer" brands. A word of caution in switching is necessary. A recent study has shown that when smokers have switched to cigarettes lower in nicotine content, more cigarettes of the new brand are smoked almost exactly in such proportion as will bring the daily intake of nicotine up to the amount formerly consumed.

So far in this chapter on battle strategy, we have tried to: (1) break down the complex problem of smoking into smaller, manageable bits, and (2) to acquaint the smoker with the essential nature of the smoking habit. One more element of basic strategy needs to be discussed. It will be so much easier for the smoker, once he has committed himself to give up the habit, to give up smoking for just one day at a time. He is not to think about next week, or even tomorrow. His foremost aim is to get through this one day, even if he must achieve this limited victory hour by hour, one hour at a time, or every hour, minute by minute. Again, the smoker can see the strategy of breaking up a time interval into small units that can be easily handled because he has not set for himself an unattainable goal. He has succeeded in getting through a half a day without smoking. He is still alive and is not going to be much worse off for finishing out the rest of the day.

All the smoker must concentrate on is getting through one day. That's all. If he feels that he must resume smoking, he will resume tomorrow, but it will be tomorrow—not today. One of the advantages of a non-smokers' clinic, or school, is that of having a definite short-interval goal, the next meeting, to shoot at. The smoker knows that if he can hold out until then, he will be among friends and in a non-smoking situation where he will get relief, for at least a few hours, from the nagging of his habit. Without the help of a clinic, the smoker must set up his own time-interval schedule. We cannot emphasize too strongly the importance

TABLE I

# Tar and Nicotine Levels for 22 U.S. Cigarette Brands

| CIGARETTE BRAND | (NICOTINE IN Mg.) | (TAR CONTENT IN Mg.) |
|---|---|---|
| **LUCKY STRIKE** | | |
| 100 mm. Filter Menthol | 1.03 | 19.4 |
| 100 mm. Filter | 1.28 | 20.6 |
| King Size, Filter Menthol | 1.22 | 20.7 |
| King Size, Filter | 1.33 | 21.7 |
| Reg. Size, Non-filter | 1.55 | 26.4 |
| **KOOLS** | | |
| King Size, Filter Menthol | 1.56 | 20.2 |
| Reg. Size, Non-filter | 1.84 | 26.3 |
| **MARLBORO** | | |
| King Size, Filter (hard-pk.) | 1.34 | 20.4 |
| King Size, Filter | 1.41 | 20.7 |
| 100 mm. Filter | 1.38 | 20.9 |
| King Size, Filter Menthol | 1.72 | 24.4 |
| **WINSTON** | | |
| King Size, Filter | 1.29 | 20.4 |
| King Size, Filter (hard-pk.) | 1.22 | 20.8 |
| 100 mm. Filter Menthol | 1.66 | 25.2 |
| 100 mm. Filter | 1.74 | 26.7 |
| **RALEIGH** | | |
| King Size, Filter | 1.53 | 20.8 |
| King Size, Non-filter | 1.98 | 27.8 |
| **VICEROY** | | |
| King Size, Filter | 1.43 | 21.0 |
| King Size, Filter (hard-pk.) | 1.43 | 21.4 |

| CIGARETTE BRAND | (NICOTINE IN Mg.) | (TAR CONTENT IN Mg.) |
|---|---|---|
| **CAMEL** | | |
| King Size, Filter | 1.26 | 21.0 |
| Reg. Size, Non-filter | 1.39 | 24.2 |
| | | |
| **CHESTERFIELD** | | |
| King Size, Filter Menthol | 1.19 | 21.0 |
| King Size, Filter | 1.16 | 22.4 |
| Reg. Size, Non-filter | 1.20 | 22.7 |
| King Size, Non-filter | 1.54 | 28.6 |
| | | |
| **SALEM** | | |
| King Size, Filter Menthol | 1.36 | 21.1 |
| 100 mm. Filter Menthol | 1.74 | 27.0 |
| | | |
| **PALL MALL** | | |
| 100 mm. Filter Menthol | 1.47 | 22.3 |
| 100 mm. Filter | 1.56 | 23.1 |
| 95 mm. Filter Menthol (hard-pk.) | 1.45 | 25.9 |
| King Size, Non-filter | 1.60 | 27.1 |
| 95 mm. Filter (hard-pk.) | 1.58 | 28.1 |

| CIGARETTE BRAND | (NICOTINE IN Mg.) | (TAR CONTENT IN Mg.) |
|---|---|---|
| **DOMINO** | | |
| King Size, Filter | .71 | 15.0 |
| **PARLIAMENT** | | |
| King Size, Filter (hard-pk.) | 1.01 | 15.8 |
| King Size, Filter | 1.05 | 16.1 |
| **KENT** | | |
| King Size, Filter | 1.09 | 17.4 |
| 100 mm. Filter | 1.46 | 23.4 |
| **TAREYTON** | | |
| King Size, Filter | 1.07 | 17.5 |
| 100 mm. Filter | 1.23 | 20.2 |
| **L & M** | | |
| Reg. Size, Filter | .93 | 18.5 |
| King Size, Filter (hard-pk.) | 1.06 | 19.4 |
| King Size, Filter | 1.15 | 21.3 |
| 100 mm. Filter Menthol | 1.44 | 25.3 |
| 100 mm. Filter | 1.41 | 25.6 |
| **PHILIP MORRIS** | | |
| King Size, Filter | 1.29 | 18.9 |
| King Size, Filter Menthol | 1.28 | 20.0 |
| Reg. Size, Non-filter | 1.45 | 22.7 |
| King Size, Non-filter | 1.79 | 28.1 |

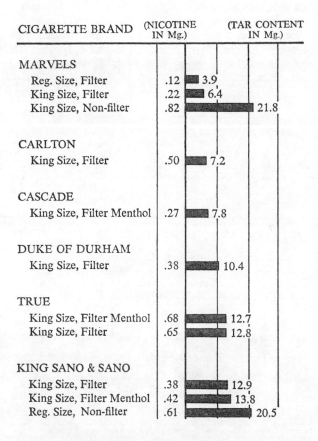

| CIGARETTE BRAND | (NICOTINE IN Mg.) | (TAR CONTENT IN Mg.) |
|---|---|---|
| **MARVELS** | | |
| Reg. Size, Filter | .12 | 3.9 |
| King Size, Filter | .22 | 6.4 |
| King Size, Non-filter | .82 | 21.8 |
| **CARLTON** | | |
| King Size, Filter | .50 | 7.2 |
| **CASCADE** | | |
| King Size, Filter Menthol | .27 | 7.8 |
| **DUKE OF DURHAM** | | |
| King Size, Filter | .38 | 10.4 |
| **TRUE** | | |
| King Size, Filter Menthol | .68 | 12.7 |
| King Size, Filter | .65 | 12.8 |
| **KING SANO & SANO** | | |
| King Size, Filter | .38 | 12.9 |
| King Size, Filter Menthol | .42 | 13.8 |
| Reg. Size, Non-filter | .61 | 20.5 |

From official U.S. Federal Trade Commission figures taken from the Jan.-Feb. 1968 issue of National Interagency Council on Smoking and Health Newsletter.

and effectiveness of this strategic maneuver. This certainly does not mean that the smoker is going to sit by the clock and watch the hours go slowly and painfully by. He is going to employ a number of other stratagems that will hopefully make him forget the passing or, rather, the standing still of time. The time-interval strategy is used only when all else fails and he has been caught with his defenses down.

# Chapter 6
## Tactics and Weapons

### PSYCHOLOGICAL WARFARE

"What do I do when I begin to feel the need for a cigarette?" is what the smoker who has decided to quit smoking wants to know. The answer is that there are many things he can do. The important thing is that he does whatever is best to do at the moment. This depends on the circumstances he finds himself in. For instance, how long has he been off cigarettes? What was his daily consumption? What symptoms has he had? What measures has he used so far to avoid a resumption of smoking?

No one can give a smoker specific help or advice in advance. No two smokers react the same even in similar circumstances. We can, however, outline a general strategy, as was done in the preceding chapter, and give more or less specific suggestions that have helped others in similar situations. If you will study carefully the battle plans that follow, most of your difficulties will be greatly minimized. If you are really conscientious in following them, the problems may never arise.

### I  *Avoid the Smoking Situation*

A good commander never looks for a fight unless he is sure that the odds are overwhelmingly in his favor. Otherwise, he will always try to avoid a fight. The smoker should likewise avoid the enemy when he can, until he is absolutely sure he has the enemy licked. Therefore, he should avoid, whenever and wherever possible, those situations that have called for a smoke in the past. For example:

(a)  Difficult, critical, tension-producing situations at work or at home (for the first few days), keeping in mind that non-smokers have these same tensions, but are not at the same time burdened also with "smokers'" tension.

(b)  Situations associated with his smoking habits such as drinking, watching TV, relaxing after dinner, or reading the newspaper.

(c)  Smoking situations at evening social affairs, cocktail parties, playing bridge, poker, or bowling in the company of other smokers.

If the foregoing suggestions seem to the inveterate smoker to be unattainable or unrealistic goals, and that he would have to lock himself in the attic, or tape his mouth with adhesive to achieve them, may we remind him that we have suggested that he avoid the smoking situation *whenever* possible. He certainly cannot avoid them all at all times. He must do whatever his determination and ingenuity permit him to do. Every single cigarette avoided is a victory, and if tomorrow is not as successful as today, you are still ahead.

The essential point to keep in mind is that breaking the cigarette habit is a learning process. The possibility of failure must be regarded only as a temporary interruption of the learning process. Remember the lady in the first chapter who was on her thirteenth try! The Seventh-day Adventists have discovered a powerful psychological tactic that simply rules out any possibility of failure, and we recommend its use to our readers. Instead of saying, "I'm not going to smoke any more," they say, "I choose not to smoke." You see, a smoker may easily fail to live up to his vow not to smoke again and risk discouragement, but he can always live up to the promise of the second statement!

## II  *Substitutions for Smoking*

It is obvious that the smoker trying to avoid the smoking situation will have to substitute other activities to fill the time he formerly took up with smoking. Many smokers who had quit successfully up to three months or more have confessed that they resumed the cigarette habit out of sheer boredom! This is a danger that must be provided for. They had failed to provide good, permanent substitute activities to take up their smoking time. The substitutes we offer here will tide you over the withdrawal period, but it will be up to you to find permanent worth-while activities to fill up your free time later. Right now we have two general suggestions, one for the men, and one for the ladies. For the men, now is the right time to undertake all those little repair jobs around the house you have been putting off; for the ladies, now is a good time to catch up on your sewing. These are good activities because they will keep your hands busy. Chapters 8 and 9 contain numerous specific suggestions for cigarette substitutions and their proper application.

## III  *Psychological Warfare*

Psychological warfare is a modern term for an old, old, military tactic. It is a powerful weapon in any war, and the smoker can use it to good advantage in his fight to break the cigarette habit.

(a) Thought control—We prefer the term "thought control" to the psychological term "suppression." Instead of "banishing" the thought of a smoke when it arises, we prefer that the smoker "lead" his thoughts away from it. Both "suppression" and "banish" suggest the need of a greater force of will power than is necessary to achieve effective application of this principle. It gives the picture of a smoker sitting down gritting his teeth and repeating, "I will not think of smoking." Needless to say, this probably will not work.

The essential feature of the thought-control tactic demands an immediate switch of the thought of a smoke arising in the mind. With a little practice and planning it is easy to do. This is the principle. Read it carefully.

The *instant* any idea of smoking enters the mind, even before it has a chance to develop in any manner, shape, or form, it must be eliminated by substituting other prearranged ideas. Here is an example of how it works.

A friend of ours, in the midst of a nervous breakdown, would be beset occasionally by spells of depression. As an ardent fisherman, the greatest thrill of his life was to hook "into" a whopper of a fighting fish and land it skillfully, using only light tackle. As a means of countering these periods of depression, he began immediately switching his thoughts to the struggle of landing his fish, and his spell of depression never had a chance to get started. The point is, of course, that he fended off unpleasant thoughts by having a substitute *ready*. He went even further, and worked up half a dozen substitute "ideas" for any emergency. The smoker can do the same. Everyone must have similar exciting memories that he has relived in the past and can relive again as a substitute in "a smoking emergency."

Here is one thought-control device you may use effectively until you develop several of your own. Let us assume the urge to smoke suddenly comes to mind. You say, "Hold it! I've got some figuring to do. I want to know exactly how much money I have saved on cigarettes since I quit." If you don't have a pencil handy, do your calculation mentally, down to the last penny. Now figure it for one week, two weeks, a month, a year. So far, you have "led" your thoughts from smoking to mathematics. You now lead your thoughts from mathematics to consumer goods that your savings could buy, things that you've always wanted, but thought you could never afford. The purpose of all this is to get your mind off the subject of your need for a smoke. The craving for a cigarette is not constant and will depart as suddenly as it comes. Do not expect this one trick to pull you through every time. It is a tactic or gimmick for use until you develop some thought-control ideas of your own. Remember also that the thought-control bit is an emergency measure until you can get your mind and hands busy with some real activity.

(b) Delaying tactics—Another tactic that is an important weapon in warfare, and which the smoker can use to good advantage, is the delaying tactic. The idea is to stall off your urge to smoke, to play for time. You have put off your urge to smoke many times before, when other urgent business had to be disposed of first, so you can do it again.

Your habit waited before until you were ready, so it will wait again now until you are ready. If your urge has suddenly crept up on you before you could get your thought control working, you merely say, "You'll have to wait a minute. I have something important to do right now." And you proceed to do a number of things you have planned in advance for this emergency (repairs, sewing). Just take it easy. Keep stalling for time. Two hours to bedtime, and you've got it made for this day! Always think in terms of killing the next few hours, sometimes even minutes. Your urge to smoke will not nag you constantly. It will leave you as suddenly as it comes, and the longer you put it off, the intervals between urges will become longer and longer.

Here, then, in review, are the three weapons you will be using to free yourself from your cigarette habit. Fix them in your memory.

The Avoidance of the Smoking Situation
Substitutions for Smoking
Thought Control and Delaying Tactics

Two suggestions are offered on the most effective use of these weapons. A good commander does not squander all his ammunition at once. He uses only as much as he needs for the moment, and holds the rest in reserve. Hold some weapons in reserve for unexpected emergencies. Secondly, meet each emergency as it comes along. Don't worry about tomorrow, or the next hour, or the next fifteen minutes. Always remember, the worst will be over in a few days.

# Chapter 7
## Count Down to Blast Off

### PREPARATIONS FOR Q-DAY (QUITTING DAY)

One of the important messages we have tried to convey in these pages is that giving up cigarettes should not be undertaken lightly. It should be done very deliberately. Impulsive, dramatic, or impatient crash programs to quit rarely succeed. The more thought and planning you give to this "adventure for health and freedom" the greater your chances of success will be.

This chapter relates to the very important element of preparing yourself, physically and psychologically, for a specific date, which we will call Q-Day (quitting day). Q-Day should be set by you sometime in the very near future with the exact date to be determined by your individual circumstances. Consider, for instance, the conditions under which your smoking habit is most compulsive or least compulsive. Choose a date that will include a time period that will be as free of personal tension-producing problems as possible. Also, a time when your social calendar can spare you from gatherings where smoking is the order of the day or evening.

Some sacrifices and concessions to your normal daily schedule will have to be made. After all, consider the rewards awaiting your success in this venture. Consider also that your sacrifices are only temporary, in force only as long as it takes to reroute certain habit patterns that now regulate your daily smoking routine. And finally, keep in mind that a conscientious adherence to the suggestions that follow will lessen the periods of sacrifice and inconvenience.

Having now set the exact date for Q-Day, one week or

two at the most in advance, you are ready to make another decision relating to what method of stopping is best for you. You have two alternatives: stopping "cold turkey" on Q-Day or "tapering off" from now until Q-Day. "Cold turkey" is a sudden and complete break from cigarettes that has been used successfully by many, even heavy smokers. The ability to drop the cigarette habit abruptly in this fashion does not necessarily bespeak superior character or will. It reflects rather a personality trait. It may also of course reflect the action of a smoker whose doctor has issued a strong warning to cease and desist at once, or else. Since you are the person best acquainted with your capabilities in following through with a prearranged plan, you must choose that method which you think will work out best for you. If you choose to taper off, we can suggest several options, with each option having the goal of reducing your cigarette consumption either to zero, or at least to half your daily quota, by Q-Day.

(a) Every time you reach for a cigarette ask yourself, "Do I really need this smoke or is this impulse merely a reflex action related to an automatic habit?" You may be surprised to learn how many cigarettes you have been lighting in this fashion without regard for conscious need.

(b) Decide arbitrarily that you will smoke only on the even or odd numbered hours of the clock.

(c) Be selective in the choice of certain cigarettes that seem more important to you than others. If you can learn to do without these for one or two weeks before Q-Day, you will already have licked the worst of your habit when Q-Day arrives.

(d) Finally, try switching brands. For some, this has helped during the tapering-off period.

Other preparations are in order for Q-Day. Your cigarette habit is a resourceful opponent with a bagful of tricks, and you must be prepared with proper counter-measures for every emergency. Again, proper attention to anticipated difficulties will pay off handsome dividends in lessened discomfort. The preparations with additional suggestions can be summarized in this countdown.

*important*

10. Definite date set for Q-Day.

9. Decision on "cold-turkey" or "tapering-off" method.

8. If "tapering-off" option is used, follow suggestions described previously.

7. Put all cigarettes, ash trays, book matches, cigarette lighter out of harm's way. (Don't throw away ash trays. Snuff boxes and cuspidors have become collectors' items.)

6. Lay in a supply of the following:

Vitamin A supplements to minimize your withdrawal discomfort.

Vitamin B complex (best form is wheat germ, available in any supermarket). This helps to steady the nerves as you deprive your system of nicotine.

Fresh fruits of all kinds.

Large quantities of canned fruit juices. These will help to flush your system of nicotine residues.

Snacks, all kinds: olives, celery, carrots, dried fruits, crackers, mints, hard candies, or gum.

5. Provide yourself with a supply of easy reading material, such as *Reader's Digest*. Light reading to take up smoking time is good for coffee breaks. Crossword puzzles and other similar distracting activities are also helpful.

4. You must also provide yourself with activities that will keep your hands busy. Stim-U-Dents, soft chewable toothpicks, will accomplish this. We made some suggestions earlier about house repairs for men and handwork or mending for women when they are home. If you play a musical instrument the problem of restless hands is solved. You must make every effort to help yourself in this matter. Nor must you wait until panic strikes before you start to think about what to do. You must be ready in advance to meet this and other emergencies.

3. Plan to get up earlier for a few days to avoid the tensions of hurrying through breakfast and rushing to work.

2. Arrange in advance for a baby-sitter so you can spend the first night or two at a movie or other entertainment or activity where smoking is not permitted.

1. Spend as much time sleeping as you can. The impulse to smoke during sleep is a rare occurrence.

0. Blast off for Q-Day!!!

# Chapter 8
## In Orbit

### SEVEN-DAY HEALTH BINGE

And now you are in orbit! Our analogy between a space exploration and the smoker's attempt to win freedom from his cigarette habit may seem a bit fanciful. There are, however, a number of striking parallels in both operations. Perhaps the most striking parallel is the importance given to preparatory details. If the smoker, for instance, has neglected to check all of the essential steps leading to countdown, he had better postpone the event and wait for better weather.

Secondly, the smoker's entry into a strange new world will require such changes in daily routine and habits, including diet, that he may feel disoriented and therefore uncomfortable for a while. However, the exhilaration of this new adventure will help to minimize the discomforts, and the thoughts of a new life ahead will keep his aim steady and his determination firm.

In the following hour-by-hour suggestions in the one-week program to kick the cigarette habit, the reader must realize that this routine had been designed for the average smoker. This means that some suggestions may not fit his circumstances. If, for instance, the smoker is a housewife, she may be confronted with the coffee-break situation all day long. Therefore, she must be ready to adapt some of the suggestions to suit her personal requirements and use her imagination to find additional satisfactory substitutes.

### DAILY ROUTINE:

The first week of the withdrawal period calls for a strict adherence to the following daily routine. We can only approximate what a typical smoker's situation would be for a day. The individual must adapt to his own situation the particular restriction called for.

| Daily Routine (First Week) | *Cigarette Substitutes* |
|---|---|
| *NO* prebreakfast cigarette today! | Head for the shower right away, or drink a glass of cold water. |
| *Breakfast* Fruit juice (large) Cereal or boiled eggs (easy on the pepper) Whole-wheat toast Fresh fruit—any kind. *NO* coffee this morning! | Take milk or another glass of fruit juice. The coffee-cigarette combination is so deeply ingrained in the average smoker's habit it will be best to avoid coffee for a few days. |
| *After Breakfast* Do *not* sit down! Put your Stim-U-Dents in your pocket and add some fruit to your lunch box. | Brush your teeth again vigorously, this time to get rid of the taste of food. The eating-smoking habit must be disassociated for a few days. If you have a few minutes to spare, take a brisk walk. Inhale deeply and get your "lift" from some extra oxygen. |
| *The Coffee Break* A lovely, relaxing, and pleasant American custom, but right now one of the worst booby | Avoid the coffee-break situation for a few days. Substitute *any* or *all* of the following activities: Instead of |

Daily Routine
(First Week)

*Cigarette Substitutes*

traps for the would-be
ex-smoker.

coffee, drink fruit juice
or milk. (Skim milk is
recommended.) Eat fruit
or chew gum. Take a walk
in the fresh air if pos-
sible. Read this book
during break.

*Lunch*
Keep it light, with
salads, fruits, and
fruit juice or water.
Take a vitamin sup-
plement.
Do not sit down after
eating. A crowded
stomach makes breath-
ing more labored and
may trigger an urge
to smoke, since labored
breathing is associated
with the deep inhaling
of smoking.

Instead of sitting, stand
or take a walk. Inhale
deeply. Brush your teeth
if possible. If not, use
your Stim-U-Dent to re-
move the food particles.
This gives you activity
for your hands, and is
good massage for the gums.

*Midafternoon*
This is one of the
most critical times
of the day. You are
tired, and your spirits
at a low ebb. Apples,
oranges, or bananas
make good snacks.

Use the same suggestions
given for the coffee break
earlier. Also, if you have
decided to quit with an-
other smoker, get in touch
with him at this time. If
you do not need his help,
he may need yours. Ask
him how he is doing.
Even if you want to save
ammunition for later days,
don't hesitate to eat any
snacks if you must, to

| Daily Routine (First Week) | Cigarette Substitutes |
|---|---|
| | ward off the urge for a smoke. |
| *Evening Meal*<br>Fruit juice. No heavy meal with fried or spicy foods. Fruit for dessert.<br>*Still* no coffee.<br>Do not sit down. | Brush teeth vigorously after every meal for the first week. Avoid established smoking situations. Take a brisk walk in the fresh air. |
| *Evenings*<br>If you are also a TV addict, don't sit in your usual comfortable seat. A rubber ball to squeeze during commercials will keep your hands busy. Use all of your available gambits including chewing gum, toothpicks, handwork, or reading. Beware of overeating, as eating triggers the desire for smoking. | It will be easier to spend the first two nights at a movie or other entertainment where smoking is not permitted. Beware of eating afterward. Head for a relaxing bath and sleep. |

## EMERGENCY MEASURE

If a sudden craving to smoke catches you unawares, take five slow, deep breaths. Hold the last breath while you strike a match. Then exhale very slowly, blowing out the match at the very end of your exhalation. Crush the match as if it were a cigarette and pretend you have just finished a smoke. Then immediately get busy on some work, or play a game of solitaire.

## WITHDRAWAL DISTRESS

Before the end of the third day, the would-be ex-smoker may have experienced some periods of discomfort. The symptoms, which are primarily physical, range, as we said earlier, from mild in some individuals to severe in others. They may take many forms, depending on the smoker's own physical and psychological make-up and the length and strength of his addiction. Some people get feelings of increased nervous excitability such as restlessness, insomnia, anxiety, tremor, or palpitation. Others will experience diminished excitability such as drowsiness, amnesia, impaired concentration, and diminished pulse. None of these disturbances is harmful. If you develop any feelings of anxiety about them, a talk with your doctor will reassure you.

To those who have won this part of the fight painlessly, we offer our congratulations, with the hope that they will not fall victim to overconfidence. To those for whom the distress has been extreme we offer our sympathies, and some words of comfort. First of all, no one ever said that breaking the cigarette habit would be easy, nor did those who are having difficulties believe that it would be. We do believe that their discomfort is less than it would have been without the suggestions offered in this book.

We believe also that the severity of their symptoms has revealed to them the high degree of their subjugation to the cigarette habit, and that this realization should strengthen their resolve to accept nothing less than a total victory over a slavish habit that can bring such affliction. For such an investment in discomfort, they are entitled to all the rewards that cessation from cigarette smoking will eventually bring.

# Chapter 9
## Weightlessness

### THE BATTLE OF THE BULGE

Astronauts weigh nothing while in orbit and weigh less on their return to earth than before they started. There is no mystery to this. If smokers trying to break the cigarette habit watched their diets as carefully as astronauts, they would have no weight problems. As a general rule, however, people put on weight for a while after giving up cigarettes. It is not hard to understand why this should be so. In the first place, all foods smell and taste so much better after not smoking for a while, that there is a natural temptation to eat more. Secondly, many smokers in the process of trying to get off cigarettes reach for a bite to eat when the urge for a smoke hits. Furthermore, the elimination of the appetite-depressing effects of nicotine returns to normal the rhythmic motion of the stomach muscles, and this accounts for increased appetite.

Some individuals have reported that they have gained weight without adding to their calorie intake. This phenomenon can be explained as the beneficial result of a healthier bodily function, whereby an improved metabolism is providing a better utilization of the former smoker's normal calorie intake. Overweight is a known health hazard, but many smokers have been led to believe that the health risk of overweight is on a par with the health risk of smoking. Nothing could be farther from the truth. As one heart specialist put it, "A gain of ten pounds in a one-hundred-sixty-pound man is no serious health risk. Only an eighty-pound gain in weight in a one-hundred-sixty-pound man would bring his health risk from overweight to the level of his risk from continued smoking."

The most sensible course for the would-be ex-smoker is to tackle one problem at a time. The major problem for him now is to kick the cigarette habit, even if he has to gain some weight to do it. The overweight problem can be taken care of later. Besides, there is another difference between the health risks of smoking and the possible health risks of overweight, which can be stated in this way. The smoker's added weight cannot escape his notice. What his clothes or mirror won't tell him, his bathroom scales will. The damage to the heart and lungs from cigarette smoke is on the inside, where he cannot see them  One day, without warning, when it is too late to repair the damage, the smoker will get the grim message of irreparable damage to his internal organs.

To keep weight increase to a minimum, the smoker has two choices. He must watch his added calorie intake. For snacks as cigarette substitutes, dried fruits, celery sticks, carrot strips, and chewing gum are preferable. The alternative is to take steps to burn up the added calories by a systematic program of exercise. May we emphasize, in summing up, that giving up cigarettes will not result in added weight for anybody. Eating food in excess of one's requirements will result in added weight for everybody. It would be a serious mistake for any smoker to accept the false belief that his only choice is either to continue to smoke to keep his weight normal, or to give up cigarettes and gain weight. If smoking would keep people slim, why do overweight smokers outnumber overweight non-smokers, which they do! The only salvation of any overweight is to take steps to learn the principles of weight control. The national organizations of such groups as TOPS (take off pounds sensibly) and the Weight Watchers have developed successful programs to help individuals to control their weight.

Since many healthful approaches to weight control are available, it makes no sense to inhale the poisons of cigarette smoke in the belief that this will guarantee a slender figure.

# Chapter 10
# Down to Earth

### HOW TO BE AN EX-SMOKER FOR LIFE

Sooner or later, the would-be ex-smoker must come back to earth, the earth of reality, the earth of smoke-filled conference rooms, theater lobbies, restaurants, and night clubs; the earth of tension, frustration, and boredom. In the previous chapter we noted that the excitement and glamour of a new venture (getting off cigarettes) and the exhilaration of victory achieved will sustain the new ex-smoker for a time. We are all too familiar with the natural tendency in all human endeavor for any period of sustained high-level effort to slack off, to be followed by a period that has given many successful ex-smokers their greatest moments of trial and difficulty. It is the time when the slightest yielding to temptation (a single puff will do it) can destroy in one instant all the satisfactions and rewards of a hard-won battle.

The three formidable enemies of the new-fledged ex-smoker are tension, frustration, and boredom. If he is not on his guard, after having won the opening rounds of his fight, any one of these three evils will put him right back on Tobacco Road. Listen to this sad story: "I was off cigarettes for six weeks. Work got slack, I was bored. As soon as work picks up, I'm going off again." Here's another: "The baby got sick. I was worried and nervous. I just had to do something." Many people go back to cigarettes without even such understandable reasons. They have said, "I was just bored at the moment. I didn't intend to resume regular smoking, mind you." But they are hooked again nevertheless.

What are the proper antidotes for tension, frustration, and boredom? Certainly not cigarettes. Why take poison into your system as an antidote for another set of poisons; for these three evils are "real" poison to the recent ex-smoker. Avoid them, and you will be an ex-smoker for life. How to avoid them? Again, only general suggestions can be made, which must be adapted by the ex-smoker to the needs of the moment.

We have already warned about overconfidence, especially on the part of those who got off the habit with a minimum of difficulty. If they feel that they have now proved they can go off cigarettes any time they choose, *they will always choose to go back on again.*

Restrictions on the avoidance of smoking situations, drinking coffee, and resuming regular diets should be relaxed gradually, and only when the ex-smoker is certain that any impulse to light up will not be beyond his control. Let him not be alarmed, after he has been "off" cigarettes for some time, even several months, that an occasional strong urge for a smoke will suddenly hit. This is par for the course. Expect it to happen, and a good part of its torment will be lost. The urge to smoke lessens with the passing of time, and the periods between urges become longer.

As we explained earlier, the recurring urges to smoke are no longer a craving of the body for nicotine. The smoker has starved that craving completely after the first week or two. Later urges are longings based on psychological recall of old habit patterns associating smoking with pleasant occasions.

The ex-smoker will easily recognize the period when he has finally achieved the status of a confirmed non-smoker. As long as he feels any sense of regret at having stopped, or feels the loss of a former pleasure, as long as he feels envy for his still-smoking friends for the pleasures they seem to be enjoying, he will ever be vulnerable to relapse and must therefore continue to be constantly on guard. When finally he gets to the point, as he eventually must, that his feeling of envy changes to sadness for his smoking friends, and he can say in silent and grateful prayer, "Thank God, I don't have to do that any more," he will be safe, and no temptation to smoke will ever assail him again.

In the meantime, until the smoker reaches that happy state, much work remains to be done. Activity is the keynote for the near future. Fill up your spare time with so much work and play, you'll have little time to think about smoking. For the immediate present, we have suggested house repairs for him and mending projects for her.

Over the long pull, you must look around for a long-term mental or physical activity. Hundreds of worth-while hobbies are available, such as projects with the children and their friends. Here are two examples of what can be done to fill your life and time with new interests. Some ex-smokers of our acquaintance have become interested in making Christmas presents for their families and their friends instead of buying them. This personal touch in Christmas giving makes the best kind of present, and the making of them can fill many happy hours. Don't worry about not being in the right mood. The Christmas-present industry operates the year round. Its busiest season is in the spring. Another example of what has been done by a group of ex-smokers to help themselves to resist the temptation to resume smoking is their formation of a non-smokers club. This group meets monthly and plans programs for local service clubs and churches to encourage and help other smokers to give up the habit. You may be sure that having committed themselves in such fashion, it is unlikely they will ever go back to smoking. And a very important point not to be overlooked is that these folks are having a lot of fun being involved in what they consider to be a worth-while endeavor.

A last word. If, from time to time, you feel sorry for yourself that you are missing some fun by not smoking, look about you, as you work or play, at your co-workers and friends who are not smokers. By latest count there are seventy million of them. There may seem to be more smokers than non-smokers, but as someone has said, they just smell louder. Look at those who are not smoking. Do they look as though they are missing any pleasure by not smoking? Do they seem dejected, downcast, or cheerless? Or are they not just as gay and carefree as the rest of the smoking crowd and having just as much fun? We learned just the other day over the phone that one of our best friends has given up cigarettes, off for six weeks now after a number of unsuccessful tries. We cannot describe how our admiration of her has soared. We do not exaggerate when we tell you that as an ex-smoker, you will be the envy of all your smoking friends and acquaintances. Certainly you will be proud of your achievement. You are a complete man (or woman) again. Your soul is your own, unburdened by a slavish habit. You have reason to be proud. There are few accomplishments in life that match this! No wonder that the former smoker remembers the exact date of his emancipation from cigarettes, long after he has forgotten other highlights of his life. Ask any ex-smoker the date he quit smoking. He may have trouble remembering the date of his wedding anniversary, but that date he will always remember.

It is hardly necessary in closing to mention the other rewards in store for the smoker for his effort and success in giving up cigarettes, namely, yearly dividends in good health, and paid-up health insurance for a longer and happier life. If, as a smoker, you still have this journey to make, we wish you good luck. The rewards are worth it!

# Section II
# Smoking and Health Program Ideas

## Chapter 11
## Helping Others

### A CHALLENGE TO COMMUNITY LEADERS

The magnitude of the smoking and health problem in terms of the widespread use of cigarettes suggests that any significant reduction in cigarette consumption and its consequent yearly toll in disabling diseases and excess deaths can be achieved only through total mobilization of all available community resources. The organized and responsible health agencies, public and voluntary, at federal, state, and local levels, have instituted many educational programs aimed mainly at reducing the number of current cigarette smokers and the number of new smokers who daily join their ranks.

There is another invaluable community resource that must also be utilized if a total effort is to be directed toward these goals: namely, the resource of the responsible, dedicated individual who operates as a professional worker or as a private citizen. One of the chief strengths of a democracy is the opportunity it gives to everyone in the exercise of his responsibility as a citizen to make his unique contribution to the good life of the community.

The high esteem with which the physician, the teacher, the clergyman, and the health professional are regarded in the community indicates how influential such individuals can be by participating in educational programs directed at discouraging the practice of smoking, especially among the young. The doctor can warn his patients who are beginning to show symptoms of cigarette-induced illnesses that they had better stop smoking. He may suggest to all of his smoking patients, whether their symptoms are cigarette induced or not, what heavy risks of future illness they run by continuing to smoke. He may also involve himself, if he can spare the time and feels strongly about it, as a leader or participant with other community leaders, in a smoking cessation clinic. For the assistance of the physician in such a project, or for anyone else who is adequately trained, the authors have included a chapter in this section dealing with the organization of such a clinic. Above all, and this counsel is directed to all who wish to influence others with regard to the harmful effects of tobacco, the doctor's own example as a non-smoker will help most effectively in bringing about any changes in attitudes and behavior toward smoking among his patients.

The teacher's influence in discouraging potential smokers among the youngsters under his guidance can hardly be exaggerated. The teacher of science or health will have many opportunities to introduce the subject of smoking and its bad effects on health as part of his regular program. Teachers of other subjects who, besides following regular courses of study, use the world about them as a useful text will also find or make opportunities to inform their pupils of the dangers of cigarette use, especially the folly of using the cigarette as a quick and easy entree to adulthood. Again, the teacher's personal example as a non-smoker will speak more eloquently than any sermon he can preach in molding the proper attitudes and habits among his protégés.

Many state and local departments of education have included lesson units on smoking and health as part of the regular health and science programs. If resource material is not available to him, the teacher may find the listing of available resource and educational material in this section of the book valuable. Three sample Smoking and Health Units designed for elementary, junior high, and senior high school teachers are also included.

Other influential leaders in many communities, such as social workers, business executives, youth organization leaders, may contribute much by taking part in educational activities in this important health movement.

We all know of the important contributions that they as individuals can make in this vital area of educating people about the hazards of cigarettes. Every individual can help. We heard recently of a school nurse in a local junior high school who personally enlisted signed pledges not to begin smoking from six hundred youngsters in her school. It is with the purpose of helping individuals to help themselves, and additionally to help others, that this book has been written. Certainly, the non-smoking missionary will want to familiarize himself with the first section of the book, that he may learn to understand the smoker's problem, and thus be in a better position to help. On the other hand, the smoker who has used the first section of the book successfully to break his cigarette habit may now, in the role of ex-smoker, use the material in the second half as a text for his potential anti-smoking efforts.

## SUGGESTIONS ON TEACHING
## ABOUT SMOKING OR HEALTH

1. Instruction in the classroom related to the health implications of smoking must be planned and conducted with the view of leaving the final decision to the pupil. Since the desired behavior will be carried out independent of the school setting, personal decision making should be the appropriate goal.

2. Experience has shown that scare tactics and moral preachment are the least effective mechanisms in inducing changes in attitude about smoking. Unemotional presentation of factual data on the medical, biological, and chemical effects of smoking on the human organism has so far proven to be the most effective approach.

3. A realistic approach to any effective behavior changes among youngsters must recognize the strong counter influences and pressures exerted by the pupil's peer groups, the permissiveness of smoking in the family setting, and the general acceptability of smoking as a social custom, to say nothing of the smoking habits of teachers themselves.

4. Whether the teacher is a smoker or a non-smoker, it is no longer appropriate for him to be indifferent or neutral on the desirability of young boys and girls starting to smoke.

## HINTS FOR THE
## ELEMENTARY SCHOOL TEACHER

### A. *Introduction:*

1. General goals in teaching the health hazards of cigarette smoking are the same at all age levels: namely, to induce present smokers to give up the habit and to prevent smoking in those who have not yet started. Since the desire for adult status constitutes the chief motivation for youngsters to smoke, every effort must be directed to counter this pressure by upgrading the status of the non-smoker. More specific, immediate objectives and procedures are listed below. It must be kept in mind, though, that the considerations of a variety of teaching situations and the time availability of resource materials will require considerable planning and adaptation for effective teaching.

### B. *Objectives:*

1. To discover the extent of interest in the subject of smoking.

2. To discover the extent of information on the widespread use of cigarettes and their harmful effects.

3. To discover the extent of misinformation, half-truth, fallacies, and myths regarding same.

4. To gather, with the help of pupils, all pertinent facts relating to the subject, and convey, in language appropriate to the age level, the salient facts regarding the health hazards of smoking.

### C. *Procedures:*

In grades five and six, students begin to be curious about, but are not as yet committed to, the habit of smoking. The importance, therefore, of early instruction to develop attitudes that will reduce their susceptibility to adopt the habit can hardly be exaggerated.

1. Gather information on smoking habits and attitudes of parents, using a simple questionnaire as the following, being sure to stress the anonymous nature of the survey:

*Questionaire:*                              Mother        Father
                                             yes  no       yes  no

    Do you smoke?

    Have you tried to stop?

    Do you think you could stop?

    Do you wish you had never started?

    Do you think smoking is harmful to your health?

    Do you approve of young people smoking?

2. Tabulate and discuss the results of this survey.

3. Have pupils list the advantages and disadvantages of smoking to the individual and to society (loss due to fires, and economic loss because of disabled smoker, premature death, etc.).

4. Discuss the above, touching on the validity of adult status and sophistication as stated advantages.

5. Have students examine the appeals used in cigarette advertising. Discuss the effectiveness and validity.

6. Review the mechanism of heart and blood vessel function, and convey in simple terms the effect of nicotine on them.

7. Review the mechanism of the respiratory system and the adverse effects on this of the tar in cigarette smoke.

8. List the organs affected by smoking and list the cigarette-induced illnesses that result.

D. *Resource Materials:*

1. Film—"Huffless, Puffless Dragon" available from the American Cancer Society.

2. Bulletin board—for charts, posters, articles, and displays.

3. Booklets, pamphlets, and other handout materials are listed separately at the end of Section II of this book.

HINTS FOR THE JUNIOR

HIGH SCHOOL TEACHER

A. *Introduction:*

1. Reliable surveys show that five thousand youngsters daily join the ranks of regular smokers, 10 per cent in the

seventh grade, escalating to 50 per cent in the twelfth grade. It may be presumed that the subject of smoking and health will assume increasing importance in school health curricula as time goes on. It will be helpful, therefore, to begin any teaching program on this subject with a survey questionnaire as a guide to test the effectiveness of the instruction as revealed in subsequent changes in smoking attitudes and behavior. Again, stress the anonymity of personal response to the questions.

B. *Objectives:*

In addition to the general objectives listed previously for lower grades, we include the aim of obtaining pertinent information regarding the smoking behavior and attitudes of the pupils.

C. *Procedures:*

1. Distribute the foregoing sample questionnaire to all pupils, again stressing the fact that no identification of respondent is necessary or desired.

2. Tabulate and discuss results.

3. Follow the procedures listed under grades five and six, adapting the depth and breadth of the discussion to the age and understanding levels of the class.

D. *Resource Materials:*

1. Film—"Smoking and You" available from the American Heart Association.

2. Debates may be based on these suggested topics:
"Cigarette Advertising Should Be Banned."
"Cigarette Advertising Should Be Restricted."
"Cigarette Taxes Should Be Used for Education on Smoking and Health."
"Stricter Enforcement on Sale of Cigarettes to Minors Is Necessary."

3. Simple experiments demonstrating harmful effects of cigarette use may be undertaken (see suggestions listed in the section "Hints for the Senior High School Teacher").

4. Bulletin board—for articles, charts, and displays.

## HINTS FOR THE
## SENIOR HIGH SCHOOL TEACHER

A. *Objectives:*

1. Questionnaire, tabulation, and discussion.

2. Follow procedures suggested for lower grades, adapting the activities to age and sophistication levels of students.

B. *Resource Materials:*

1. Film—"Is Smoking Worth It?" available from the American Cancer Society.

2. Debates in class or planned for assembly program on subjects suggested earlier.

3. Campaign to elevate status of non-smoker by wearing of appropriate pins by smokers pledging to stop.

4. Development of scientific displays, especially by science students, demonstrating harmful effects of cigarette use.

### SUGGESTED SCIENTIFIC EXPERIMENTS

1. *Purpose*—To demonstrate the effect of smoking upon the heart rate.

*Procedure*—Non-smoking students may use voluntary smokers as subjects. Pulse should be taken two or three times previously to establish a base-line accuracy. Pulse then should be taken after third or fourth puff. After cigarette is finished, pulse should be taken every fifteen minutes until pulse rate returns to normal.

*Conclusion*—Calculated increased volume of blood pumped on basis of twenty cigarettes (one pack) and seventy cc. of blood each beat will demonstrate extra burden on heart, resulting in lessened life expectancy.

2. *Purpose*—To demonstrate constriction of blood vessels and consequent lowered temperatures of extremities as a result of inhaled nicotine.

*Procedure*—Tape thermometer to hand of subject and take reading prior to smoking. Take reading after first inhalation to note how quickly the temperature drops. Normal reactions should show a range of a 3- to 9-degree temperature drop as result of nicotine from one cigarette.

*Conclusion*—Cigarette smoke results in restricted blood flow to extremities as demonstrated by lowered surface temperature. (The same effect can be demonstrated visually by observance of capillaries in ear of rabbit after injection of nicotine solution into blood stream.)

3. *Purpose*—To demonstrate the presence of tar compounds in cigarette smoke.

*Procedure*—(Simple demonstration) Ask smoker to blow a generous puff of smoke (not inhaled) through a hankerchief or a piece of Kleenex. Then ask smoker to blow a generous puff of *inhaled* smoke through a different section of the handkerchief or Kleenex filter.

*Conclusion*—The almost negligible brown stain left by the inhaled smoke as compared with the dark brown stain left by the uninhaled smoke demonstrates that the tar compounds of inhaled cigarette smoke remain in the lung passages.

4. *Purpose*—To demonstrate the presence of tar compounds in cigarette smoke.

*Procedure*—Construct a simple smoking machine by inserting a Buchner funnel with smoking tube over a suction flask. The wet filter paper insert will trap the tar compounds as the smoke is sucked through it.

5. *Purpose*—To demonstrate the toxic (poisonous) effects of the chemicals in cigarette smoke.

*Procedure*—Direct the smoke from the cigarette-smoking apparatus through a beaker filled with water taken from the fish tank. After three cigarettes have been consumed, transfer a goldfish from the fish tank to the beaker. The fish will show loss of control over its movements, and he must be removed almost immediately to avoid death.

6. *Purpose*—To demonstrate the fallacy that cigarette smoking relaxes the smoker, as claimed by many.

*Procedure*—Construct a tremor-testing apparatus. A series of twelve holes, ranging from ½ to 1/16 inches in diameter are drilled through a square of 1/16-inch metal plate. A wire from a bell is attached to the plate. A second

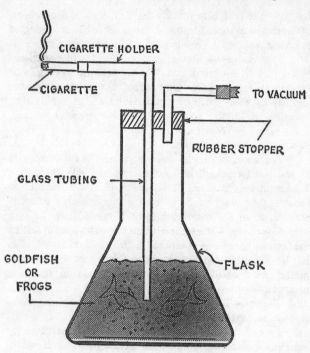

wire is attached to a needle which completes the circuit and rings the bell when contact is made with the edge of the hole. The object of the demonstration is to compare the smoker's muscular control of the needle in avoiding contact with the plate before and after smoking.

# Chapter 12
## Organizing a Withdrawal Clinic

### HOW TO CONDUCT A CIGARETTE SMOKING
### CESSATION CLINIC

Smoking cessation clinics, also called withdrawal or dissuasion clinics, have been growing in popularity in this country as more and more smokers are deciding to rid themselves of the cigarette habit. Although some smokers are able to break the habit on their own, many have failed. The clinic method, using education and some sort of group therapy, has proved to be an effective way of helping cigarette smokers break the habit. The clinic is also a useful device in providing an immediate action program for those who are in present need of help. Until other long-range educational programs can be developed, the clinic may also represent a symbol of the community's concern to provide what service it can for its members.

The *modus operandi* of a cessation clinic as described in this booklet, together with accompanying suggestions and recommendations, is based on a survey of the current literature on the subject, plus the practical experience gleaned from the operation of a number of cessation clinics by the research team of the Philadelphia Smoking and Health Project during the past few years. It is expected that the general principles laid down with regard to the various aspects of clinic organization and procedures may be adapted to meet the varied requirements of the individual smoker's special needs, the problems or characteristics of a particular smokers' group, and the resources available.

## ORGANIZATION

One dedicated energetic organizer, preferably a physician, clergyman, psychologist, or health educator, plus half a dozen smokers ready to be weaned from the cigarette habit, can be the basis of a smokers' cessation clinic. If there are more of either category, so much the better. It is assumed that no organization would be attempted short of such a minimum, and that clinic sessions would always include physicians or other professionals as participants. If large numbers of smokers are desired, recruitment measures appropriate to the resources at hand must be undertaken. Random recruitment has its dangers, however, and a screening procedure is recommended. A personal interview, some sort of preliminary information meeting prior to the clinic sessions, or a nominal charge for the clinic will help to eliminate certain categories of poor risks who would drain energy from the clinic that could better be employed for the more serious. Poor risks would include such individuals as the merely curious individuals with insufficient motivation, those individuals who are looking for a magic pill to do the job, and individuals unable to consistently attend the scheduled clinic sessions. Such individuals generally tend to blame the clinic for their failures as a convenient excuse for their continued smoking.

## MEETING SCHEDULES

A second indispensable in the operation of a smokers' clinic, besides a leading spirit, is a meeting place. Again depending on the size of the group and the resources of the community, almost any meeting room conveniently accessible and of appropriate size would be suitable. The number and spacing of meetings must be subject to the convenience of the individuals of the group, but, it can be assumed that no schedule will suit everybody. A minimum of five and a maximum of ten two-hour sessions are recommended. It is also suggested that the first five sessions be held on week days within a two-week period, since the greatest difficulties of the new ex-smoker will be experienced during that time.

The idea of a preparation period for Q-Day (quitting day) is becoming recognized as beneficial in the clinic procedure. Either a preliminary meeting or educational material sent through the mail in advance of the clinic should be utilized to: (1) prepare prospective participants psychologically for the withdrawal symptoms they may have, and (2) give them some opportunity to assemble certain supplies to be used as cigarette substitutes in the early days of their smoking cessation. Chapter 7, "Count Down to Blast Off," gives additional details on preparation for Q-Day.

## CLINIC

Experience indicates that the most successful smokers' cessation clinics combine two objectives in their operation: (1) Education of the smoker about the health hazards of smoking and the physiological and psychological aspects of the smoking habit, and (2) The involvement of the clinic participant in some sort of group interaction and discussion sessions.

### A: EDUCATIONAL FEATURE

A typical two-hour evening session would include a one-hour educational period involving the use of a filmstrip, films, or lecture by an informed local physician or health educator. The first lecture might be devoted to a review of the objectives of the clinic, an over-all picture of the extent of the health hazards of cigarette smoking, and explanation of the nature of the smoking habit, the general principles of group therapy, and the necessity of habit retraining.

In conjunction with films and slides, other lecture sessions should cover the chemistry and pharmacology of tobacco smoke, the effects of cigarettes on the respiratory and cardiovascular systems, the incidence of lung cancer for smokers, the comparison of over-all death rates for non-smokers and smokers, and the improved statistical picture available to the individual giving up. In addition, specific suggestions relating to combatting withdrawal symptoms, using gimmicks, devices, and diets that will help the smoker over the initial phases of cessation should be included within the first two weeks of the clinic. If the clinic participants are primarily parents, the involvement of youngsters in a special session geared for this purpose seems to be effective. Finally, a session should be devoted exclusively to the problem of weight control as the participants tend to gain some weight because of additional caloric intake.

The educational sessions can also be supplemented by auxiliary literature that the clinic participants can read at home. A great deal of reading material on smoking and health has been developed, and local branches of the American Cancer Society, Heart Association, and Tuberculosis & Health Association will usually fill any requests for materials without cost. The Philadelphia Smoking and Health Project has developed a Smoking and Health Resource Booklet which lists by agency the various booklets, pamphlets, films, and slides that are available. Additional copies of this book may be useful as texts for home reading for clinic members.

A very effective adjunct to the regular program of education might be the participation of one or more ex-smokers who will give brief personal case histories of their smoking problems and their eventual success. If such guests are also "graduates" of earlier clinic programs, so much the better. Also, the presence, as a guest, of a recovered hospital patient, who was a victim of a tobacco-induced ailment, would be an effective device. A brief ceremony involving the awarding of a diploma or pin would have a most salutary effect on the potential ex-smokers in the group. It is further suggested that some sort of diploma or pin be given to successful quitters at the six-month date of his success.

## B: GROUP DISCUSSION

The second part of one typical session should be devoted to the "treatment" of participants via the use of group discussion and interaction. The size and number of groups again will depend on the number of clinic participants and the availability of experienced group-discussion leaders. If small groupings of individual participants are not possible, it is suggested that time be allowed for group discussion on a mass basis, since the discussion of problems occurring during the weaning period is an essential part of the program. Since so much of the success of this group-discussion phase depends on the skill and personality of the leader, we shall discuss both the factors of leadership and the technique in more detail.

## C: THE SKILLED LEADER

Although skillful leadership in group dynamics is an essential in general to successful group therapy, understanding of a few basic principles and a genuine desire to understand and help people with their individual problems will often compensate for technical shortcomings. An individual who meets most of the following criteria should be successful as a group-discussion leader in a smokers' clinic. (1) If possible, he should be an ex-smoker. This status gives him a sympathy for the problems of the struggling ex-smoker that one who has never smoked is rarely able to achieve. (2) He should be well informed on the health hazards of cigarette smoking and the physiological and psychological aspects of the smoking habit. (3) He must be able to direct, without seeming to lead, the discussion toward certain clearly defined goals: namely, to produce changes in attitude and behavior through the group process. He must be able to do the foregoing without dominating the discussion. He must restrain the extroverts in the group and draw out the introverts, and develop a rapport both among the group members themselves and between them and himself. (4) Finally, and most important, he must be interested in the individuals in his group, not only as subjects for psychological or sociological study, but as human beings whose problem will respond to the dynamics of individual or group therapy in direct proportion to the genuine personal interest evidenced by the therapist.

### D: GROUP INTERACTION

The essence of group therapy and the basis for its success have been defined thus: "The misinformed are corrected; the fearful discover that their fears are groundless; and the discussants reinforce each other, not only by finding that they have problems and experiences in common, but also by providing answers the others may lack." However, the processes by which free discussion can be channeled into effective and progressive reinforcement and final control of modified and acceptable habit patterns are not automatic. Much will depend on how skillfully the leader can refine the raw experiences of the individuals of his group into patterns of behavior that will win acceptance of the group and thereby achieve a group allegiance and loyalty. At this point a smoker who is still struggling to master his habit can, out of a sense of loyalty to the group, be helped by a new determination not to "let down" or fail his friends.

Another objective of group interaction that should not be overlooked by a leader who is intent on exploiting all the possible benefits of group dynamics is the active involvement of each individual within the group, not only in his own personal smoking problem, but also in the smoking problems of his newly found friends in the group. The group leader who can sit back and be a spectator to a half dozen individuals, who forget their own problems for twenty minutes to ponder seriously the problems of one of their group, to offer advice, to suggest alternatives, or even admonish when necessary can feel a sense of pride in his accomplishment.

### WRAP-UP

One final thought—many smokers come to a clinic to seek an easy solution to their problem. The trick is to hold them long enough to get them to understand that the help they will need to break the cigarette habit must eventually come from within. This, of course, is the clinic's basic function—to help people to help themselves. It is the only help that the clinic can really give. With it, many smokers have succeeded, and without it, many have failed.

# Chapter 13
## Resource Materials on Smoking and Health

### INSTRUCTIONS AND COMMENTS

This chapter has been prepared to assist various groups and individuals who wish to utilize certain smoking and health visual aids—pamphlets, books, films, and displays—that have been developed by various agencies in recent years. Provided is a convenient, alphabetical compilation of most of the resource material that is currently available. The costs, if any, are also noted. It is important that the reader understand that all materials desired should be ordered from the *local* affiliate of the agency concerned. This information can generally be obtained from the telephone directory. It is anticipated that smoking and health programs, concepts, and materials will be undergoing constant change and revision. As new materials become available they will be appended to this chapter whenever possible.

## RESOURCE MATERIALS AVAILABLE FROM
## YOUR LOCAL CANCER SOCIETY

### A. *Pamphlets*

1. *Cigarettes: Are the Facts Being Filtered?* A reprint from *Redbook Magazine* pointing out the health hazards of smoking.

2. *I'll Choose the High Road* A 4-panel leaflet designed for distribution to fifth and sixth grades em-

phasizing the relationship of smoking and physical fitness, and the health risks of smoking.

3. *Modifying Smoking Habits of High School Students*     A 10-page pamphlet by one of the leaders in the field, Dr. Daniel Horn. He discusses the problem of educating teen-agers so they do not begin to smoke.

4. *Shall I Smoke?*     A 4-panel leaflet on lung cancer which includes bar charts on lung cancer death rates and identifies cigarette smoking as the major cause of lung cancer.

5. *To Smoke or Not to Smoke*     A 6-panel leaflet summarizing some of the recently published data on smoking.

6. *Your Health and Cigarettes*     A 6-panel leaflet discussing the diseases related to cigarette smoking and what you can do to live longer and healthier.

7. *Who, Me?—Why?*     Concise summary of the risks of cigarette smoking and the benefits of quitting. Stresses the point, "Yes, you can quit," and points out it's never too late to quit and still receive the health benefits.

8. *Who, Me? . . . Quit smoking*     A pamphlet discussing why individuals should quit smoking, and how beneficial cessation will be. Offers specific advice on how to quit.

9. *A Time for Decision*     This leaflet is written to urge various community leaders to become involved in anti-smoking efforts.


## B. *Booklets*

1. *Cigarette Smoking & Cancer*     A 32-page booklet discussing the entire problem of smoking and cancer in detail.

2. *Answering the Most Often Asked Questions About Cigarette Smoking & Lung Cancer*     The

questions are concise and the answers are convincing
in this 4-fold pamphlet.

3. *The Effect of Smoking*    A 16-page reprint
from *Scientific American Magazine* of an article by Dr.
Cuyler Hammond, outstanding researcher.

4. *Smoking and Health Summaries and Conclusions*
A reprint of Chapter 4 of the Report of the Advisory
Committee to the Surgeon General of the Public Health
Service. Required reading for smokers and non-smokers
alike.

5. *Where There's Smoke*    This booklet is designed to bring information on smoking, in story form,
to persons who enjoy illustrated reading matter in
comic-book format. It is intended primarily for younger
high school students.

6. *What to Tell Your Parents about Smoking*    A
booklet for parents and children that details the relationship between smoking and certain specific diseases.

## C. *16-MM. Films*

1. *Huffless, Puffless, Dragon*    An animated 8-
minute color cartoon with sound, for children. Recommended for use in schools in grades six to nine, it deals
with pressures on children to smoke.

2. *Is Smoking Worth It?*    A motion picture produced by the American Cancer Society for senior high
and adult groups. It does an effective job of telling the
story without reliance on the scare techniques sometimes found in other films.

3. *Smoking & You*    A 12-minute English film
that comments satirically on the unglamorous aspects
of smoking.

4. *Who, Me?*    A 14-minute motion picture produced by the American Cancer Society for adults. It
examines the influence of parents on their children's
decisions about smoking.

5. *Breaking the Habit*      Sound, color, 6 minutes. Animated cartoon employing a humorous approach, showing two characters having an offbeat conversation about the cigarette smoking habit and their unsuccessful efforts to break it. Ends with straightforward message on the health hazards of cigarette smoking.

6. *The Time to Stop Is Now*      Sound, color, 4 minutes. Animated cartoon. In clear crisp cartoon drawing, this brief film explains the body's remarkable capacity for self-repair. Particular emphasis is given to the effects of stopping smoking, as related to lung cancer and heart attack.

7. *Time for Decision*      Sound, color, 20 minutes. Depicting up-to-date information on new concepts of changing smoking behavior.

## D. *Filmstrips*

1. *To Smoke or Not to Smoke*      Sound, color, 84 frames—35 mm. Included, a 15-minute record of the filmstrip text. This filmstrip is addressed directly to students in junior and senior high schools and stresses the importance of the decision, to smoke or not to smoke. The growing seriousness of lung cancer is graphically presented; research studies showing the relationship between smoking and lung cancer are explained; and the effect of smoking on normal functions of the lung is shown.

2. *The Cancer Challenge to Youth*      Sound, color, 65 frames, for grades seven to twelve. It covers the nature and history of cancer as a disease and major health problem, normal and abnormal cell behavior, diagnosis and treatment, the importance of individual responsibility for self-protection, and the type found in various fields of cancer research. Smoking studies have been used to illustrate the American Cancer Society research program.

3. *I'll Choose the High Road*    Sound, color, 59 frames, 35 mm. Includes a 15-minute record of the filmstrip text. This color filmstrip, with recorded narration, discusses the relationship between cigarette smoking and several health complications of nose, throat, heart, lungs. Cancer is not stressed but it is treated briefly and factually. Emphasis is on the importance of physical, mental, and social fitness in enjoyment of future opportunities and in meeting life's challenges. Fitness through development of wholesome habits is encouraged. The filmstrip is intended for use chiefly with pupils in sixth, seventh, and eighth grades.

## E. *Slides*

1. *Slides on Cancer Statistics*    Various slides developed by the American Cancer Society are available depicting the effects of smoking on cancer.

2. *Speech—Slide Presentation*    Complete talk and set of slides. Length about 45 minutes. Concisely presents biological and statistical evidence that smoking is a serious health hazard. Points to leadership of the American Cancer Society in research, education, community, and rational action. Devised for flexible use.

## F. *Additional Materials*

1. *Posters*    Posters and bulletin-board materials of varying sizes are available depicting the hazards of the cigarette habit.

2. *Display*    Your local Cancer Society has a 3-inch by 5-inch folding cardboard display available for use as a backdrop for smoking and health meetings or for material displays. This display is entitled, "To

Smoke or Not to Smoke," and pictorially depicts the health hazards of smoking.

3. *Lecture Flip Chart*      Your local Cancer Society has available a large flip chart with lecture outline for use by interested individuals or groups.

## RESOURCE MATERIALS AVAILABLE FROM YOUR LOCAL HEART ASSOCIATION

### A. *Pamphlets*

1. *What about Smoking & Heart Disease?*      A 4-page leaflet discussing the range of scientific evidence and smoking as it relates to certain heart diseases.

2. *What I Tell My Patients about Smoking*      A reprint of an excellent article by Howard Sprague, M.D., former president of the American Heart Association, offering advice to patients on smoking.

3. *What Everyone Should Know about Smoking and Heart Diseases*      A 4-panel leaflet that summarizes a number of medical studies that have been made, which demonstrate a statistical association between heavy cigarette smoking and death or illness from coronary heart disease. Includes a statement made by the Board of Directors of the American Heart Association.

4. *What School Children Think about Smoking*      A 4-fold pamphlet on the attitudes of California school children expressed in original posters, which show perception in their assessment of smoking as a future habit.

5. *Where There's Smoke There's Danger from Heart Disease*      A 1-page piece discussing the relationship of smoking and heart disease. Good for envelope inserts.

6. *Enjoy the Pleasures of Not Smoking*      A leaflet depicting in cartoon form the benefits of cessation of cigarette smoking.

## B. *Booklets*

1. *Cigarette Smoking & Cardiovascular Disease*
A 4-page, 8½-inch by 11-inch statement by the American Heart Association on the relationship of smoking to cardiovascular disease.

2. *Smoking, Health, and You*    Twenty-two pages of facts on smoking and health written specifically for teen-agers. Single copies free, quantities available from U. S. Government Printing Office, Washington, D.C.

3. *Your Teen-age Children and Smoking*    A 14-page booklet geared toward parents based on ideas and opinions expressed by teen-agers who attended a National Smoking and Health Conference. Single copies free, quantities available from U. S. Government Printing Office, Washington, D.C.

## C. *16-MM. Films*

1. *Smoking and You*    An excellent 12-minute film pointing out the hazards of cigarettes and the unglamorous side of smoking in a satirical vein. Developed in England but available in this country.

2. *Smoking and Heart Disease*    A 10-minute, animated, color film which discusses the relationship between cigarette smoking and heart disease.

3. *Barney Butt*    A 12½-minute color film done in cartoon style. Geared to youth. Tells about a young man with an extensive smoking habit.

## D. *Additional Materials*

1. *Posters*    Posters and bulletin-board materials of varying sizes depicting the hazards of cigarette smoking are available.

2. *Television Spots*    TV spot films discussing the risks of cigarette smoking and heart disease are available from your local office of the Heart Association. Films come in 10 second, 20 second, 30 second, and one minute lengths which make them suitable for TV spot programming.

### RESOURCE MATERIALS AVAILABLE FROM ROSWELL PARK MEMORIAL INSTITUTE

## A. *Pamphlets*

1. *Memo to Adults about Cigarette Smoking* This 6-panel leaflet, 3½-inch by 6½-inch in three colors, gives facts and figures about smoking and the effects on health. Designed for adults.

2. *Smoking . . . It's up to You*    This 6-panel leaflet, 3½-inch by 6½-inch in three colors, points up problems in starting the smoking habit and what smoking means to continued good health. Designed for teen-agers.

## B. *Booklets*

1. *Health Hazards of Smoking*    This booklet summarizes the scientific evidence that relates smoking to various health problems. It is especially useful for teachers who need factual information for classroom use. Limit of 10 copies available at no cost. More than 10 copies—$.05 per copy.

2. *Curriculum on Smoking and Health*    This pamphlet outlines two simple, basic, educational programs. One program is designed for use in grades five to seven and the other for use in grades eight through twelve. Listed are available visual aids as well as scientific experiments which can be performed by students

interested in the physiological effects of smoking. Limit of 10 copies available at no cost. More than 10 copies—$.05 per copy.

## C. *Filmstrips*

1. *The High Cost of Smoking*    This is a 52-frame, 28-minute filmstrip with descriptive lecture recorded on tape. Included also is a written script for easy reference. Designed especially for young people, the filmstrip presents the facts about smoking, lung cancer, and other smoking related diseases. Particularly good for schoolroom use. Filmstrip kit, including magnetic tape, script, packaging, and mailing—$4.75 per kit.

## D. *Slides*

1. *Lecture Slide Kit*    This set of 40 color lecture slides, 2-inch by 2-inch, 35 mm., is designed for use by physicians, teachers, nurses, and science students. A suggested lecture outline is included. Lecture slide set includes 40 slides, outline, packaging, and mailing —$8.00 per set.

## E. *Additional Materials*

1. *Posters*    Posters and bulletin-board materials of varying sizes depicting the hazards of cigarette smoking have been developed.

2. *Auto Plates*    Black and white front bumper auto plates depicting the health hazards of smoking. The 12-inch by 6-inch plate is printed on heavy metal with long-wearing, baked-on enamel. Mounting holes are prepunched for easy installation. Auto plate, including postage—$1.50 each.

3. *School Science Experiments*     Six experiments showing the physiological effects of tobacco smoke and how to collect tars from cigarettes are outlined. Designed for junior and senior high school science classes. Limit of 10 copies available at no cost. More than 10 copies—$.05 each.

4. *Matchbook Covers*     Four differently designed matchbook covers are available from Roswell Park with each cover cleverly satirizing the hazards of cigarettes—$.01 each.

## RESOURCE MATERIALS AVAILABLE FROM YOUR LOCAL TEMPERANCE SOCIETY

### A. *Pamphlets*

1. *How to Stop Smoking*     Describes ten steps in a program to eliminate smoking written by Wayne McFarland, M.D.—$1.25 per 100; $10.00 per 1000—plus postage.

2. *Will One Million Really Die?*     Examines and rebuts the denials by cigarette companies that are seducing young people through ads.

3. *The Winner*     A monthly publication (except June, July, and August) written in story form for teenagers. Uses illustrations and pictures—$.75 for single subscription (9 issues); $.45 per subscription in clubs of 30 or more to one address. Write for bulk prices.

### B. *Booklets*

1. *Lung Cancer and Its Relationship to Smoking* Sixteen pages. A most convincing statement of the evidence. Power packed and highly recommended. Written by Alton Ochner, M.D.—$.10 each; $4.00 per 100; $17.50 per 500.

2. *Should a Boy Smoke?* Twelve pages by Harold Shryock, M.D. What every teen-age boy should read—$3.00 per 100.

3. *Smoke Signals* A monthly, 4-page publication designed to develop public interest in today's extensive research on the effects of tobacco. Single copy—$.10; subscription, $3.50 per 100; $25.00 per 1000.

4. *Why Quit Smoking?* Sixteen pages by Paul Harvey, ABC News Analyst. He tells you why. Recommended. A reprint. Single copies—$.05 each; $4.00 per 100.

## C. *16-MM. Films*

1. *Beyond a Reasonable Doubt* A 25-minute color film showing the effect of the smoking habit on the heart. The effect of smoking on an expectant mother and her unborn child is graphically depicted. Available from American Temperance Society.

2. *Cancer by the Carton* A 30-minute color film. Here is medical evidence in story form. A magazine editor searches for the facts on smoking and health. He is faced with tremendous economic and personal obstacles before his editorial board will approve the publication of his finding. Outstanding physicians appear in the film.

3. *One in 20,000* This 30-minute color film offers the true story of a man who is told by a chest surgeon that he has lung cancer and must undergo surgery. The operation is real and all the sights and sounds are authentic. A powerful, though somewhat grisly, documentary.

4. *Time Pulls the Trigger* This 23-minute color film shows how carbon monoxide, one of the poisons in tobacco smoke, affects red blood corpuscles, and how nicotine causes smaller blood vessels to constrict.

A doctor describes the relationship of smoking to lung cancer, and states plainly that smoking adversely affects the heart and other organs and tissues of the body.

5. *Up in Smoke*    A 23-minute color film showing how half-truths and deceptive claims are forced upon the public to protect the economic interests of the tobacco industry.

RESOURCE MATERIALS AVAILABLE FROM
YOUR LOCAL TUBERCULOSIS ASSOCIATION

## A. *Pamphlets*

1. *Cigarette Smoking—The Facts*    An 8-panel leaflet opening with a series of questions: "Would you buy a product advertised to leave a bad taste in your mouth? Smell up your clothes? Make your breath foul? Give you that sluggish feeling? Discolor your fingers and your teeth? Damage your health?" Then it proceeds to provide the reader with facts on smoking and health.

2. *Don't Let Your Health Go up in Smoke*    This 6-panel 8½-inch by 3¾-inch leaflet points out that cigarette smoking is a factor in coronary heart disease, chronic bronchitis, emphysema, and lung cancer. It emphasizes the fact that cigarette smokers risk death sooner than non-smokers.

3. *Excessive Cigarette Smoking*    A small 4-panel leaflet that emphasizes the three major dangers of excessive smoking and urges the reader not to smoke at all, or at least to cut down.

4. *Filter the Facts Before You Smoke*    Scientific evidence linking various illnesses with smoking is summarized in this 4-panel, 8½-inch by 3-inch leaflet.

5. *Let's Face It, Pal*    This is a 4-panel leaflet spe-

cifically aimed at patients with respiratory disease. It points out that smoking does a well person no good and can well prove fatal to patients with respiratory complaints.

6. *Really Want It?*     A 4-panel leaflet indicating the damage smoking does, while enumerating the benefits of reduction and abstention.

7. *The Logical Move*     A 6-panel leaflet points out the dangers of smoking and gives some hints on how to go about quitting.

8. *U. S. Government Wants You to Know*     A 4-panel leaflet discussing the labeling act.

9. *Here Is the Evidence*     A humorous leaflet that attempts to discourage people from starting the cigarette habit.

## B. *Booklets*

1. *Cigarette Smoking, Cigarette Advertising, and Health*     A 10-page reprint by R. S. Mitchell, M.D. from the *Journal of School Health*. Reviews the facts of tobacco and health and contrasts research conclusions with advertisers claims.

2. *Problems of Changing Attitudes and Actions on Smoking*     A 15-page pamphlet in two parts. Part One is described in the title. Part Two is concerned with smoking and the adolescent peer culture.

3. *Cigarettes and Health*     A Public Affairs pamphlet of 20 pages giving a clear, concise summary of all of the health problems relating to the smoking habit. Available from Public Affairs Pamphlets, 381 Park Avenue, New York, N.Y.—$.25 per copy with substantial reductions in price for larger quantities. Single free copies are available from your local Tuberculosis Association.

## C. *16-MM. Films*

1. *Smoking and You*    A 12-minute film that comments satirically on the unglamorous aspects of smoking. Developed in England but excellent for use in this country.

2. *Tobacco and the Human Body*    Sound, black and white, 15 minutes. Analyzes the contents of tobacco smoke; demonstrates some of the physiological effects of smoking; and sums up the factors to be considered in deciding whether or not to smoke.

3. *Point of View*    A 20-minute film designed for high school students. This film uses satire as a method. It has been recommended for several film awards.

## D. *Filmstrips*

1. *Nature's Filter*    Color, 55 frames, 35 mm. Script included. Based on a lecture by Dr. Richard H. Overholt, Director of Over Thoracic Clinic in Boston. This filmstrip compares the body to a machine and the lungs to a filter. It describes the effects of the smoking on the filter (lungs) and on the pipes and tubes (arteries) of the body. It shows a non-smoker's lung and a smoker's diseased lung and asks, "Which filter will you have?"

2. *Cigarettes and Health*    A 93-frame strip with record; running time, 17 minutes. Designed to stimulate all educators to teach young people about the dangers of cigarette smoking. Developed by the National Interagency Council on Smoking and Health.

## E. *Additional Materials*

1. *Posters*    Posters and bulletin-board materials

of varying sizes depicting the hazards of cigarette smoking have been developed.

2. *Exhibits*     Several large exhibits are available. They have been designed with various groups in mind.

## RESOURCE MATERIALS AVAILABLE FROM
## MISCELLANEOUS SOURCES

### A. *Pamphlets*

1. *Cigarettes and the Schools*     Eight pages for parents, teachers, and students. What the schools are doing in view of the release of the Surgeon General's report. Available from the Publication—Sales Section, National Education Association, 1201 16th Street N.W., Washington, D.C. 20036—35 for $1.00.

2. *Cigarette Smoking*     A 6-page memo to adults stating some facts uncovered by recent studies and what can be done. Available from N. Y. State Department of Health, Albany, N.Y.

3. *The Facts on Teen-age Smoking*     A 2-page reprint from *Parents' Magazine* of October 1960, by Leona Baumgartner, M.D. Prudent parents should not ignore this information. Available from the Parents' Institute, 52 Vanderbilt Avenue, New York 17, N.Y.

4. *Smoking Facts You Should Know*     An 8-page leaflet giving the facts on smoking and health as they apply to the individual smoker. Available from the American Medical Association, Chicago, Ill.—$.05 per copy; discounts for larger purchases.

5. *Smoking and the Heart*     A 4-page leaflet for adults. All the facts are here. Available from the United States Government Printing Office, Washington 25, D.C.—$.05 each; $2.00 for 100 copies.

6. *Smoking, It's up to You*     A leaflet for young people. The decision to smoke will affect one's whole

life. Here's why. Available from N. Y. State Department of Health, Albany, N.Y.

7. *Ten Little Smokers*     An exercise in cartoons and verse tells why smoking is harmful to health. Aimed at teen-agers and adults. Available free from Smoking and Health Research Project, Castor Avenue and Lycoming Street, Philadelphia, Pa. 19124.

8. *Cigarette Smokers: You Are Gambling with Your Life!*     A 4-panel leaflet showing the odds against the smoker, and the odds in favor of the non-smoker. Available free from the Smoking and Health Research Project, Castor Avenue and Lycoming Street, Philadelphia, Pa. 19124.

9. *Smoking: The Schools' Responsibility*     A brochure urging teaching personnel to discourage teenage smoking. Order from the National Education Association, 1201 16th Street N.W., Washington, D.C. 20036—$1.50 for 100 copies.

## B. *Booklets*

1. *Cigarettes and Health*     A Public Affairs pamphlet of 20 pages giving a clear, concise summary of all of the health problems relating to the smoking habit. Available from the Public Affairs Pamphlets, 381 Park Avenue, New York, N.Y.—$.25 per copy with substantial reductions in price for larger quantities.

2. *Cigarette Smoking and Health*     A review of research by the California State Department of Public Health. A summary of opinion and a proposal for action. Available from California Department of Public Health, 2151 Berkeley Way, Berkeley 4, Calif.

3. *Should We Believe Everything We Are Told About Tobacco?*     Available from Anti-Tobacco Center of America, Inc., 366 Fifth Avenue, New York, N.Y.

4. *Smoking and Health*     A 24-page booklet to be

used as a resource unit for teachers. Prepared by several health agencies and available from Lankenau Hospital, Department of Health Education, Lancaster and City Line Avenues, Philadelphia, Pa. 19151. MI 9-1400.

5. *Smoking and Lung Cancer*    A 26-page booklet discussing in detail the relationship of smoking and lung cancer. Also answers some common questions asked by the public. Available from the National Clearinghouse on Smoking and Health, Public Health Service, Washington, D.C. 20201.

6. *The Health Consequences of Smoking*    A 200-page evaluative summary of the state of knowledge covering 1964–mid-1967. A Public Health Service Review, obtainable–from the Superintendent of Documents, U. S. Government Printing Office, Washington, D.C. 20402, Publication No. 1696–$.60 per copy.

7. *Teen-agers & Cigarettes*    A 4-page discussion answering teen-agers' questions about the smoking habit. This reprint is available from Changing Times, 1729 H Street N.W., Washington, D.C.

8. *Summary of the Report of The Surgeon General's Advisory Committee on Smoking and Health* Available from the National Clearinghouse for Smoking and Health, Public Health Service, Washington, D.C. 20201.

9. *How to Keep Your Child from Smoking*    A booklet containing some practical suggestions parents can follow to discourage youngsters from smoking. Available from the National Clearinghouse on Smoking and Health, Public Service, Washington, D.C. 20201.

10. *You Can Quit Smoking*    This booklet is geared to teen-agers who smoke and want to quit. Some twenty-five experts in fields of medicine, edu-

cation, and psychology have made contributions to this booklet. Available from U. S. Government Printing Office, Washington, D.C.—$.15 per booklet.

11. *Your Teen-age Children and Smoking*　A 14-page booklet suggesting how parents can help teen-agers quit smoking. Includes comments by teen-agers. Fifty copies free if ordered through Children's Bureau. Additional copies—$.15 each from the Government Printing Office, Washington, D.C.

12. *Facts for Teen-agers—Smoking, Health, and You*　A 22-page booklet that gives medical evidence and answers questions about teen-age smoking. Fifty copies free if ordered through Children's Bureau. Additional copies—$.15 each from the Government Printing Office, Washington, D.C.

13. *You Can Quit Smoking: Young Smokers Aren't Really Hooked*　A 19-page booklet for teen-agers who smoke and want to quit. Fifty copies free if ordered through Children's Bureau. Additional copies—$.15 each from the Government Printing Office, Washington, D.C.

14. *Smoking: The Schools' Responsibility*　A position statement urging teaching personnel to discourage student smoking—$1.50 per 100 copies.

15. *Cigarettes and the Schools*　A leaflet discussing the problem of student smoking on school grounds and the development of school smoking education programs—$1.00 for 35 copies.

Both are available from the National Education Association Publications Sales, 1201 16th Street, N.W., Washington, D.C. 20036.

## C. *16-MM. Films*

1. *Too Tough to Care*　An 18-minute color film for grades nine to twelve. A light-hearted satire which deglamorizes cigarette advertising and exposes at-

tempts to manipulate teen-agers. Produced for the Marin Medical Society and California Medical Assoc. Obtained through distributor, Lawren Productions, 1433 Wooster Avenue, San Mateo, Calif.

2. *The Drag*    A 9-minute color film made in 1965. An animated characterization of "Mr. Modern Smoker" and the psychosocial nature of his habit; this film is appropriate for teen-age and adult audiences. It is available for a $6.00 rental fee from Contemporary Films, 267 W. 25th Street, New York, N.Y. 10001. Developed by the Department of National Health and Welfare of Canada.

3. *Cigarettes and Health: A Challenge to Educators*    A 17-minute film with 93 color frames, made in 1966. Designed to stimulate teachers, school administrators, and other concerned adults to establish effective smoking education programs in the schools. The filmstrip is available free from state and local chapters of most NIC member agencies and for purchase at $3.00 from Training Films, Inc., 150 W. 54th Street, New York, N.Y. 10019. Developed by the National Interagency Council on Smoking and Health.

4. *Getting Through*    A 22-minute black and white film, made in 1967. Presents the problem of smoking to young people as a paradox—society's acceptance and promotion of the habit, and medical science's rejection of it as a health hazard. Puts the responsibility for decision on the teen-ager himself. Developed by the Public Health Service and available free from the National Audio-Visual Center, Public Health Service, Chamblee, Ga. 30005.

## D. *Slides*

1. *Smoking and Health Slides*    A set of 120 slides, 35 mm., depicting the hazards of smoking. The slides are devided into four categories: (1) Car-

toons and Satire, (2) Medical, (3) Statistical, (4) Withdrawal Clinic. Sample presentations and the booklet "How to Conduct a Smokers' Cessation Clinic" are supplements available with the slides. These materials are available with the slides from the Smoking and Health Research Project, Room 540 Municipal Building, Philadelphia, Pa.

2. *Smoke and Science*     A slide talk available on a loan basis to pharmacists and health-education groups from the American Pharmaceutical Association, 2215 Constitution Avenue, N.W., Washington, D.C. 20037.

## E. *Additional Materials*

1. *Posters*     Posters and bulletin-board materials of varying sizes have been developed depicting the hazards of the cigarette habit. Check with your local affiliates to ascertain which are available.

2. *Exhibit*     Large two-sided 5-inch by 10-inch exhibits are available from the Philadelphia Smoking and Health Research Project. One section displays the chances that smokers take when they decide to smoke cigarettes, and the other section depicts the non-smokers' chances for good health. Two smaller table-top displays are also available.

## F. *Additional Resource Materials Available from U.S. Government Sources*

1. *NO SMOKING!*     A kit of the following 5 publications for youth, youth leaders, teachers, and parents:

*Your Teen-age Children and Smoking*     Gives parents some suggestions on how to help children avoid or stop smoking.

*Smoking, Health, and You—Facts for Teen-agers*
*You Can Quit Smoking—Young Smokers Aren't Really*
*Hooked*     Illustrates how to quit and why.
*Why Nick the Cigarette Is Nobody's Friend*     A cartoon
explanation for elementary students.
*A Light on the Subject of Smoking*     Geared to upper
elementary students.

Schools and organizations can obtain up to 50 copies
of the kit or obtain each item free from the U. S. Children's Bureau, Washington, D.C. 20201. Quantities
can be bought from the Superintendent of Documents,
U. S. Government Printing Office, Washington, D.C.
20402.

2. *The Facts about Smoking and Health*     Summarizes for the layman the latest information linking
smoking to specific diseases.

3. *What We Know about Children and Smoking*
A discussion of the psychosocial aspects of smoking
to help parents, teachers, and other concerned adults
understand the problem of why young people smoke
and what to do about it.

4. *Smoking and Illness*     Points out that smokers
have higher rates of illness, disability, and days lost
from work due to chronic conditions caused by smoking than do non-smokers.

5. *How to Keep Your Child from Smoking*
Gives practical suggestions to parents.

6. *Cigarette Smoking—Chronic Bronchitis and Emphysema*     Presents the evidence linking smoking
with these diseases.

7. *Cancer of the Lung*     Discusses smoking as
the major cause of lung cancer and points out that the
best prevention is not smoking.

8. *The Health Consequences of Smoking*  1967
A 130-page technical review of the newest evidence
linking cigarette smoking to illness.

Single copies and small quantities of the above are available from the National Clearinghouse for Smoking and Health, National Center for Chronic Disease Control, 4040 N. Fairfax Drive, Arlington, Va. 22203.

# Section III
## The Health Hazards of Cigarettes

### Chapter 14
### Questions and Answers on Smoking

#### INTRODUCTION

The first reports on the health hazards of cigarette smoking back in 1953 naturally created considerable gloom among the officials of the cigarette industry. One of the spokesmen of the industry, however, observed that there was no need to panic, remarking, "People are not going to give up a habit just because it is bad for them."

We have commented earlier on the lack of concern by some people for their own health. People of this type couldn't be less interested in reading about the diseases and the death risks involved in the use of cigarettes. But for those serious readers who are concerned about their health and want to know the exact extent of the risks they must accept in continuing to smoke, we are providing in this section a more or less complete summary of the principal diseases associated with cigarette smoking, along with the mortality risks involved. All of the facts were taken from the blue-ribbon advisory committee's report to the Surgeon General of the United States Public Health Service as well as from research studies that have been published since the release of the report in January of 1964. Included also in this section are comments on the value of filter cigarettes, the possibility of a safe cigarette, the relative importance of air pollution as a health hazard, and the hazard that women are exposed to when they smoke cigarettes. The information that follows is given as answers to questions generally asked about the health hazards of cigarette smoking.

### HOW DID THE SURGEON GENERAL'S REPORT DEVELOP AND WHAT BACKGROUND INFORMATION IS AVAILABLE?

The Public Health Service is the principal federal agency concerned broadly with the health of Americans and is headed by an individual given the title of Surgeon General who is appointed by the President. In 1959 the Public Health Service assessed the then available evidence linking smoking with health and made its findings known to health officials and the public. The 1959 data dealt primarily with the relationship of cigarette smoking to the development of lung cancer. Much additional information accumulated after 1959. Prompted by a reporter's question at a press conference, the late President Kennedy requested that the Surgeon General develop a report to the people on the possible hazards of cigarettes. Accordingly, in 1963 the Surgeon General appointed an advisory committee which included individuals drawn from *all* pertinent scientific disciplines and charged them with the responsibility of reviewing and evaluating all available data with a view toward coming up with conclusions and recommendations. After working for more than a year this committee reported its findings to the Surgeon General. The findings, which are simply a review of all previous studies on smoking and health, were printed in a 365-page book titled *The Report of the Surgeon General's Advisory Committee on Smoking and Health* and released to the public on January 11, 1964. The report clearly indicated cigarette smoking as a major cause or promoter of lung cancer, bronchitis, emphysema, coronary heart disease, and several other diseases. This extensive report concluded ". . . that cigarette smoking is a health hazard of sufficient importance in the United States to warrant appropriate remedial action." The conclusions of the report were accepted as the official position of the Public Health Service.

### WHAT THREE KINDS OF EVIDENCE WERE EVALUATED BY THE SURGEON GENERAL'S ADVISORY COMMITTEE ON SMOKING AND HEALTH?

#### 1. *Animal Studies*

In numerous studies, animals were exposed to tobacco smoke and tars and to the various compounds they contain. Upon follow-up, it was found that seven of the compounds were clearly established as cancer-producing (carcinogenic) agents. Other substances in tobacco and smoke, though not carcinogenic themselves, promoted cancer or produced conditions favorable to the development of cancer. Several toxic or irritant gases contained in tobacco smoke produced in experiments the kind of non-cancerous damage seen in the cell tissues of heavy smokers. This included suppression of ciliary action that normally cleanses the trachea and bronchi, and damage to the lung air sacs, mucous glands, and goblet cells which produce mucous.

#### 2. *Clinical and Autopsy Studies*

Observation of thousands of patients and autopsy studies of smokers and non-smokers showed many kinds of damage to body functions, organs, cells, and tissues. This damage occurred more frequently and severely in smokers. Three kinds of cellular changes—loss of ciliated cells, duplication of normal basal cells, and presence of atypical cells —were much more common in the lining layer of the trachea and bronchi of cigarette smokers than of non-smokers. It was reported that some of the advanced lesions seen in the bronchi of cigarette smokers were premalignant. Cellular changes regularly found at autopsy in patients with chronic bronchitis were more often present in the bronchi of smokers than non-smokers. Pathological changes in the air sacs and other functional tissue of the lungs (parenchyma) had a remarkably close association with past history of cigarette smoking.

### 3. *Population Studies*

Another kind of evidence regarding an association between smoking and disease came from epidemiological studies reviewed in the report.

In retrospective studies, the smoking histories of persons with a specified disease (for example, lung cancer) were compared with those of appropriate control groups without the disease. For lung cancer alone, twenty such retrospective studies have been made in recent years. Despite many variations in design and method, all but one showed that proportionately more cigarette smokers were found among the lung cancer patients than in the control populations without lung cancer.

Extensive retrospective studies of the prevalence of specific symptoms and signs—chronic cough, sputum production, breathlessness, chest illness, and decreased lung function—consistently showed that these occur more often in cigarette smokers than in non-smokers. Some of these signs and symptoms were found in the clinical expressions of chronic bronchitis, and some were associated more with emphysema; in general, they increase with amount of smoking and decrease after cessation of smoking. Another type of epidemiological evidence on the relationship of smoking and mortality came from seven prospective studies which were conducted since 1951. In these studies, large numbers of men answered questions about their smoking or non-smoking habits. Death certificates were obtained for those who died since entering the studies, permitting total death rates and death rates by cause to be computed for smokers of various types as well as for non-smokers. The prospective studies thus added several important dimensions to information on the smoking-health problem. Their data permitted direct comparisons of the death rates of smokers and non-smokers, both over-all and for individual causes of death, and they indicated the strength of the association between smoking and specific diseases.

Each of these three lines of evidence was evaluated and then considered together in drawing conclusions. The committee was aware that the mere establishment of a statistical association between the use of tobacco and a disease was not enough. The causal significance of the use of tobacco in relation to the disease was the crucial question. For such judgments all three lines of evidence were analyzed.

## WHAT ARE SOME OF THE DETAILS CONCERNING THE LARGE PROSPECTIVE STUDIES THAT WERE REPORTED IN THE SURGEON GENERAL'S REPORT?

The committee examined the seven prospective studies separately as well as their combined results. Considerable weight was attached to the consistency of findings among the several studies. However, to simplify the presentation, only the combined results are highlighted here.

Of the 1,123,000 men who entered the seven prospective studies and who provided usable histories of smoking habits (and other characteristics such as age), 37,391 died during the subsequent months or years of the studies. No analyses of data for females from prospective studies were available at the time of the release of the advisory committee's report.

To permit ready comparison of the mortality experience of smokers and non-smokers, two concepts were widely used in the studies—excess deaths of smokers compared with non-smokers and mortality ratio. After adjustments for differences in age and the number of cigarette smokers and non-smokers, an expected number of deaths of smokers is derived on the basis of deaths among non-smokers.

Excess deaths are thus the number of actual (observed) deaths among smokers in excess of the number expected. The mortality ratio measures the relative death rates of smokers and non-smokers. If the age-adjusted death rates were the same, the mortality ratio would have been 1.0; if the death rates of smokers were doubled those of non-smokers, the mortality ratio would have been 2.0. (Expressed as a percentage, this example would be equivalent to a 100 per cent increase.)

The mortality ratio for male cigarette smokers compared

with non-smokers, for all causes of death taken together, is 1.68 representing a total death rate nearly 70 per cent higher than for non-smokers.

In the combined results from the seven studies, the mortality ratio of cigarette smokers over non-smokers was particularly high for a number of diseases: cancer of the lung (10.8), bronchitis and emphysema (6.1), cancer of the larynx (5.4), oral cancer (4.1), cancer of the esophagus (3.4), peptic ulcer (2.8), and the group of other circulatory diseases (2.6).

For coronary artery disease alone, the mortality ratio was 1.7. Expressed in percentage form, this was equivalent to a statement that for coronary artery disease, the leading cause of death in this country, the death rate was 70 per cent higher for cigarette smokers. For chronic bronchitis and emphysema, which are among the leading causes of severe disability in this country, the death rate for cigarette smokers was 500 per cent higher than for non-smokers. For lung cancer, the most frequent site of cancer in men, the death rate was nearly 1000 per cent higher.

## WHAT WERE SOME OF THE OTHER FINDINGS EXTRACTED FROM THESE LARGE PROSPECTIVE STUDIES?

In general, the greater the number of cigarettes smoked daily the higher the death rate. For men who smoked fewer than ten cigarettes a day, according to the seven prospective studies, the death rate from all causes was about 40 per cent higher than for non-smokers. For those who smoked from ten to nineteen cigarettes a day, it was about 79 per cent higher than for non-smokers; for those who smoked from twenty to thirty-nine cigarettes a day, it was about 90 per cent higher than for non-smokers; and for those who smoked forty or more it was 120 per cent higher.

Cigarette smokers who stopped smoking before enrolling in the seven studies had a death rate about 40 per cent higher than non-smokers, as against 70 per cent higher for the current cigarette smokers. Men who began smoking before age twenty had a substantially higher death rate than those who began after age twenty-five. Compared with non-smokers, the mortality risk of cigarette smokers, after adjustments for differences in age, increased with duration of smoking (number of years) and was higher in those who stopped after age twenty-five than for those who stopped at an earlier age.

In two studies that recorded the degree of inhalation, the mortality ratio for a given amount of smoking was greater for inhalers than for non-inhalers.

The ratio of death rates of smokers to that of non-smokers was highest at the earlier ages (forty to fifty) and declined with increasing age.

Possible relationships of death rates and other forms of tobacco use were also investigated in the seven studies. The death rates for men smoking less than five cigars a day were about the same as for non-smokers. For men smoking more than five cigars daily, death rates were slightly higher. There was some indication that these higher death rates occurred primarily in men who had been smoking more than thirty years and who inhaled the smoke to some degree. The death rates for pipe smokers were little if at all higher than for non-smokers, even for men who smoke ten or more pipefuls a day and for men who have smoked pipes more than thirty years.

## WHAT MAJOR DISEASES ARE ASSOCIATED WITH CIGARETTE SMOKING?

### LUNG CANCER

Cigarette smoking is causally related to lung cancer in men with the magnitude of the effect of cigarette smoking far outweighing all other factors. The data for women, though less extensive, pointed in the same direction.

The risk of developing lung cancer increases with duration of smoking and the number of cigarettes smoked per day, and is diminished by discontinuing smoking. In comparison with non-smokers, average male smokers of cigarettes had approximately a nine- to ten-fold risk of developing lung cancer, and heavy smokers at least a twenty-fold risk.

The risk of developing cancer of the lung for the combined group of pipe smokers, cigar smokers, and pipe and cigar smokers was greater than for non-smokers, but much less than for cigarette smokers. It was also found that cigarette smoking was much more important than occupational exposures in the causation of lung cancer in the general population.

### CHRONIC BRONCHITIS AND EMPHYSEMA

According to the report, cigarette smoking is the most important of the causes of chronic bronchitis in the United States, and it increases the risk of dying from chronic bronchitis and emphysema. A relationship was shown between cigarette smoking and emphysema, but it was not established that the relationship is causal. Additional studies demonstrated that fatalities from this disease were infrequent among non-smokers. Finally, it was stated that for the bulk of the population of the United States, the relative importance of cigarette smoking as a cause of chronic bronchopulmonary disease is much greater than atmospheric pollution or occupational exposures.

### CARDIOVASCULAR DISEASE

It was established in the report that male cigarette smokers had a higher death rate from coronary artery disease than non-smoking males. Although the causative role of cigarette smoking in deaths from coronary disease is not clear-cut, the committee considered it more prudent from the public health viewpoint to assume that the established association had causative meaning than to suspend judgment until no uncertainty remained.

Although a causal relationship was not established, a higher mortality among cigarette smokers was associated with many other cardiovascular diseases, including miscellaneous circulatory diseases, other heart diseases, hypertensive heart disease, and general arteriosclerosis.

### EXACTLY WHAT ODDS DOES THE SMOKER
### PLAY IN RELATION TO PREMATURE
### DEATH RATES WHEN ONE COMPARES
### SMOKERS AND NON-SMOKERS?

Several of the prospective studies published included a table showing the distribution of the excess number of deaths of cigarette smokers among the principal causes of death. The hazard must be measured not only by the mortality ratio of deaths in smokers and non-smokers, but also by the importance of a particular disease as a cause of death.

In all seven studies, coronary artery disease is the chief contributor to the excess number of deaths of cigarette smokers over non-smokers, with lung cancer uniformly in second place. For all seven studies combined, coronary artery disease (with a mortality ratio of 1.7) accounted for 45 per cent of the excess deaths among cigarette smokers, whereas lung cancer (with a ratio of 10.7) accounted for 16 per cent.

Some of the other categories of diseases that contributed to the higher death rates for cigarette smokers over non-smokers were diseases of the heart and blood vessels, other than coronary artery disease, 14 per cent; cancer sites other than lung, 8 per cent; and chronic bronchitis and emphysema, 4 per cent. Since these diseases as a group were responsible for more than 85 per cent of the higher death rate among cigarette smokers, they should be of particular interest to public health authorities and the medical profession.

The array of information from the prospective and retrospective studies of smokers and non-smokers clearly established an association between cigarette smoking and substantially higher death rates. In this inquiry the epidemiologic method was used extensively in the assessment of causal factors in the relationship of smoking to health among human beings upon whom direct experimentation could not be imposed. Clinical, pathological, and experimental evidence was also thoroughly considered and often served to suggest hypotheses or confirm or contradict other findings. When coupled with the other data, results from the epidemiologic studies can provide the basis upon which judgments of causality may be made.

It is recognized that no simple cause-and-effect relationship is likely to exist between a complex product like tobacco smoke and a specific disease in the variable human organism. It is also recognized that often the coexistence of several factors is required for the occurrence of a disease, and that one of the factors may play a determinant role; that is, without it, the other factors (such as genetic susceptibility) seldom lead to the occurrence of the disease.

Cigarette smoking is associated with a 70 per cent increase in the age-specific death rates of males and, to a lesser extent, with increased death rates of females. The total number of excess deaths causally related to cigarette smoking in the United States cannot be accurately estimated. In view of the continuing and mounting evidence from many sources, it was the judgment of the committee that cigarette smoking contributes substantially to mortality from certain specific diseases and to the over-all death rate.

## DOES SMOKING MORE AND INHALING DEEPLY FURTHER LENGTHEN THE ODDS RELATING TO PREMATURE DEATH?

For groups of men smoking less than ten, ten to nineteen, twenty to thirty-nine, and forty cigarettes and over per day, respectively, the death rates are about 40 per cent, 70 per cent, 90 per cent, and 120 per cent higher than for non-smokers. The ratio of death rates of smokers to non-smokers is highest at the earlier ages (forty to fifty) represented in these studies and declined with increasing age. The same effect appeared to hold for the ratio of the death rate of heavy smokers to that of light smokers. In the studies that provided this information, the mortality ratio of cigarette smokers to non-smokers was substantially higher for men who started to smoke under age twenty than for men who started after age twenty-five. The mortality ratio increased as the number of years of smoking increased. In two studies which recorded the degree of inhalation, the mortality ratio for a given amount of smoking was greater for inhalers than non-inhalers. Cigarette smokers who had stopped smoking prior to enrollment in the study had mortality ratios about 1.4 as against 1.7 for current smokers. The mortality ratio of ex-cigarette smokers increased with the number of years of smoking and was higher for those who stopped after age fifty-five than for those who stopped at an earlier age.

## HOW SAFE ARE PIPES AND CIGARS?

The death rates of male cigar smokers smoking less than five cigars daily are about the same as those of non-smokers. For men smoking five or more cigars daily, death rates were slightly higher than for non-smokers in the four studies that gave this information. There is some indication that this higher death rate occurs primarily in men who have been smoking for more than thirty years and in men who stated that they inhaled the cigar smoke to some degree. Death rates for current pipe smokers were little, if at all, higher than for non-smokers, even with men smoking ten or more pipefuls per day and with men who had smoked pipes for more than thirty years.

## WHAT ROLE DOES AIR POLLUTION PLAY IN THE CIGARETTE-HEALTH RELATIONSHIP?

Since many attempts have been made to shift the blame for respiratory diseases such as lung cancer, chronic bronchitis, and emphysema from cigarettes to air pollution, it might be well to examine the subject of air pollution for a moment as a factor in the incidence of the above-mentioned diseases. Air pollution is rapidly becoming a major health problem. The weight of the solid substances of incomplete combustion that are spewed into the air of this country each day from factories and automobiles has been estimated to equal the weight of a line of bumper to bumper traffic reaching from New York to Chicago. These air pollutants contain many of the cancer-producing substances that have been identified in cigarette smoke. One of the most potent of these, for example, is benzypyrine. When an automobile is idling at a traffic light, the *fumes* from the exhaust produce twelve times as much of this substance as when the car is running at normal speeds. Therefore, there is no question that air pollution cannot be ruled out as a factor in respiratory diseases. As a matter of fact, the non-smoker living and working in the city develops lung cancer at a rate six times that of his non-smoking counterpart living in the country. All studies comparing mortality rates in the respiratory area among smokers show a higher rate for urban, as against suburban or rural dwellers. It has been said that the amount of cancer-producing chemicals in the air of such industrial centers as Detroit and Philadelphia is equivalent to the cancer-producing chemical present in the smoke of twenty-five cigarettes, and in other cities as high as the equivalent of two or two and a half packs of cigarettes.

Particles from cigarette smoke range in size from 0.1 to 0.7 micra. An average of about 90 per cent of the inhaled smoke is retained in the lungs. There is approximately 17.5 milligrams of smoke obtainable from a cigarette smoked to a butt length of 23 millimeters. In comparison, a person breathing normally for an entire day during a period of high air pollution in an industrial city would inhale only .02 to .2 milligrams of solid substance. This is one-hundredth, or a thousandth, or a range of a hundredth to a thousandth, of that obtained from one cigarette. Medical scientists have estimated that air pollution is responsible for a three-fold increase in lung cancer, but that cigarettes are responsible for a twenty- to thirty-fold increase.

One of the reasons that the breathing of atmospheric air is not the equivalent of the effects of cigarette smoke on the lungs is that polluted air is inhaled through the nose, a highly efficient mechanism for filtering out foreign substances. The smoker, on the other hand, draws the hot, tar-laden cigarette smoke directly into the lungs without the advantage of prefiltering.

This explains why scientists have not been able to produce cancer of the lung in animals. Rats exposed to cigarette smoke breathe it into the lungs through the nose, where much of the poison or chemical is filtered out. If cigarette smokers could learn to smoke through their noses rather than their mouths, they might be better off. They would still, however, be much more vulnerable to normal air pollutants than non-smokers. The combination of tars and heat inhaled in a single cigarette inhibits the ciliary or cleansing action of the lungs anywhere from one half to two hours. This means that those air pollutants that are not entirely screened out through the nose are not removed by the filtering action of the lungs, as in the case of the non-smoker. The smoker, therefore, is the victim of a double dose of cancer-producing chemicals, the first from his cigarettes and the second from the polluted air he breathes. As for the non-smoker, the polluted air he cannot avoid breathing is filtered first through his nose and then again by his lungs and returned by ciliary action to the throat and mouth. To conclude, air pollution is a factor in the incidence of respiratory diseases which affect the smoker more than the non-smoker.

## THE REPORTS ALWAYS MENTION MEN— DON'T CIGARETTES AFFECT WOMEN?

Yes, cigarettes do endanger the health of women. It is just that most studies have included only men because large numbers of women have been smoking only for twenty or so years. Even today, fewer women smoke than men and very few smoke heavily, or inhale deeply. This, then, makes it difficult for researchers to find enough women with long-term smoking habits to make a large-scale study. One research study published since the Surgeon General's report shows that the total death rates for men cigarette smokers is greater than for women smokers. Dr. Cuyler E. Hammond of the American Cancer Society

attributes this to the fact that women smoke fewer cigarettes than men, inhale less deeply, and start smoking later
in life. Common sense, though, should dictate that women
smokers will eventually face the same health risks as men
if they continue at the same pace because there is very little
difference in the cardiovascular and respiratory make-up of
the two groups.

## NOT ALL CIGARETTE SMOKERS OR EVEN ALL HEAVY SMOKERS DEVELOP PROBLEMS— HOW DOES ONE EXPLAIN THIS?

This, to our way of thinking, is not surprising at all because of the physiological individual differences related to
disease susceptibility and resistance for humans. For example, less than 2 per cent of the persons infected with
poliomyelitis virus develop paralysis—yet no one interprets
this as throwing doubt upon the virus as a cause of
poliomyelitis. You, the reader, can probably cite additional
examples of differences in severity of the more common
illnesses such as colds, coughs, and sore throats developed
by friends, which vividly describes this difference among
individuals.

## CAN A FILTER MAKE CIGARETTES SAFE?

No, a filter cannot make a cigarette absolutely safe unless a filter could be devised that is made of solid wood.
The problem for manufacturers is that filters tend to cut
down on the flavor of cigarettes. To make up for this, filter
cigarettes are often manufactured with tobacco that is con-
siderably stronger than normal. Another factor is that people seem to smoke more and inhale more deeply when
they smoke filtered cigarettes. This is done to obtain the
exhilarating feeling that comes with the inhalation of smoke
which is somewhat reduced by the filter. The same sort of
problems have been encountered by manufacturers who are
trying desperately to come up with a safe cigarette. None
can be devised which will be safe and exhilarating at the
same time.

Finally, the cancer causing and toxic factors in cigarettes are many in number, and all are not completely identified. As far as the authors are concerned, no filter can be devised to take out all of these unknown agents. The futility of a filter tip on a cigarette may be compared to the individual who wears dark glasses to protect his eyes, and who then turns on extra light so that he can see to read. Similarly, the manufacturers have added filters to meet the public demand for protection and at the same time, switched to stronger tobaccos in order to satisfy the smoker's taste.

## CAN A SAFE CIGARETTE BE DEVELOPED?

Many cigarette smokers are waiting hopefully for the development of a "safe" cigarette. Anyone who has read the previous chapters must know that a "safe" cigarette is a contradiction in terms. It would be like expecting someone to produce a safe alcohol, or safe opium. In the first place a cigarette without nicotine, or a similar potent chemical to stimulate the brain and nervous system, would not appeal to any smoker, and any "smoke" that results from the incomplete combustion of burning organic matter must result in harmful deposits of toxic substances in the respiratory tract.

A "safer" cigarette may possibly be developed, but any attempt to suggest that continued research will provide a completely "safe" one would be a cruel deception on the smoking public.

## HAS ANY ADDITIONAL EVIDENCE BEEN GATHERED ON THE HEALTH HAZARDS OF CIGARETTES SINCE THE PUBLICATION OF THE 1964 SURGEON GENERAL'S REPORT ON SMOKING AND HEALTH?

In the three and a half years since the publication of the 1964 report, an unprecedented amount of pertinent research has been completed, continued, or initiated in this country and abroad under the sponsorship of governments, universities, industry groups, and other entities. This research has been reviewed and no evidence has been revealed that brings into question the conclusions of the 1964 report. On the contrary, the research studies published since 1964 have strengthened those conclusions and have extended in some important respects our knowledge of the health consequences of smoking.

The present state of knowledge of these health consequences can, in the judgment of the Public Health Service, be summarized as follows:

1. Cigarette smokers have substantially higher rates of death and disability than their non-smoking counterparts in the population. This means that cigarette smokers tend to die at earlier ages and experience more days of disability than comparable non-smokers.

2. A substantial portion of earlier deaths and excess disability would not have occurred if those affected had never smoked.

3. If it were not for cigarette smoking, practically none of the earlier deaths from lung cancer would have occurred; nor a substantial portion of the earlier deaths from chronic bronchopulmonary diseases (commonly diagnosed as chronic bronchitis or pulmonary emphysema or both); nor a portion of the earlier deaths of cardiovascular origin. Excess disability from chronic pulmonary and cardiovascular diseases would also be less.

4. Cessation or appreciable reduction of cigarette smoking could delay or avert a substantial portion of deaths that occur from lung cancer, a substantial portion of the earlier deaths and excess disability from chronic bronchopulmonary diseases, and a portion of the earlier deaths and excess disability of cardiovascular origin.

TABLE II   Estimated years of life expectancy at various ages for males in the United States, by daily cigarette consumption

| AGE | NEVER SMOKED REGULARLY | NUMBER OF CIGARETTES SMOKED PER DAY | | | |
|---|---|---|---|---|---|
| | | 1-9 | 10-19 | 20-39 | 40 and over |
| 25 years | 48.6 | 44.0 | 43.1 | 42.4 | 40.3 |
| 30 years | 43.9 | 39.3 | 38.4 | 37.8 | 35.8 |
| 35 years | 39.2 | 34.7 | 33.8 | 33.2 | 31.3 |
| 40 years | 34.5 | 30.2 | 29.3 | 28.7 | 26.9 |
| 45 years | 30.0 | 25.9 | 25.0 | 24.4 | 23.0 |
| 50 years | 25.6 | 21.8 | 21.0 | 20.5 | 19.3 |
| 55 years | 21.4 | 17.9 | 17.4 | 17.0 | 16.0 |
| 60 years | 17.6 | 14.5 | 14.1 | 13.7 | 13.2 |
| 65 years | 14.1 | 11.3 | 11.2 | 11.0 | 10.7 |

SOURCE:   HAMMOND, E. C.  Life expectancy of American men in relation to their smoking habits. Presented at the World Conference on Smoking and Health, Waldorf-Astoria Hotel, New York City, September 11-13, 1967. 23 pp.

## WHAT IS MY LIFE EXPECTANCY AS A CIGARETTE SMOKER WHEN COMPARED TO A NON-SMOKER OF THE SAME AGE?

A valuable measure of comparison was recently calculated by Hammond from his study of over one million men and women. Life expectancy of men with respect to cigarette smokers and non-smokers is shown in tables II and III. For example, the life expectancy for a two-pack-a-day, or more, smoker at age twenty-five is 8.3 years less than the corresponding non-smoker. Men at age thirty-five and over, who smoke two or more packs of cigarettes per day, can expect between 20 and 25 per cent less life expectancy than their corresponding non-smoking counterparts. Even "light" smokers, those who smoke less than ten cigarettes per day, have from 2.8 to 4.6 fewer years of life expectancy than corresponding non-smokers.

Table III    Loss in life expectancy at various ages for
cigarette smokers compared with non-smokers

(Loss in years is also expressed as a percentage of
the total life expectancy of non-smokers)

| AGE | NUMBER OF CIGARETTES SMOKED PER DAY | | | | | | | |
|---|---|---|---|---|---|---|---|---|
| | 1-9 | | 10-19 | | 20-39 | | 40 and over | |
| | Years lost | Per cent | Years lost | Per cent | Years lost | Per cent | Years lost | Per cent |
| 25 years | 4.6 | 9.5 | 5.5 | 11.3 | 6.2 | 12.8 | 8.3 | 17.1 |
| 30 years | 4.6 | 10.5 | 5.5 | 12.5 | 6.1 | 13.9 | 8.1 | 18.5 |
| 35 years | 4.5 | 11.5 | 5.4 | 13.8 | 6.0 | 15.3 | 7.9 | 20.2 |
| 40 years | 4.3 | 12.5 | 5.2 | 15.1 | 5.8 | 16.8 | 7.6 | 22.0 |
| 45 years | 4.1 | 13.7 | 5.0 | 16.7 | 5.6 | 18.7 | 7.0 | 23.3 |
| 50 years | 3.8 | 14.8 | 4.6 | 18.0 | 5.1 | 19.9 | 6.3 | 24.6 |
| 55 years | 3.5 | 16.4 | 4.0 | 18.7 | 4.4 | 20.6 | 5.4 | 25.2 |
| 60 years | 3.1 | 17.6 | 3.5 | 19.9 | 3.9 | 22.2 | 4.4 | 25.0 |
| 65 years | 2.8 | 19.9 | 2.9 | 20.6 | 3.1 | 22.0 | 3.4 | 24.1 |

SOURCE:  HAMMOND, E. C.  Life expectancy of American men
in relation to their smoking habits. Presented at the World Conference on Smoking and Health, Waldorf-Astoria Hotel, New York
City, September 11-13, 1967. 23 pp.

## CONCLUSION

The preceding array of facts provides incontrovertible
evidence of the complete indictment of the cigarette as
the chief culprit in the development of the diseases cata-
logued. While many smokers evidence small concern over
these facts, and others still dispute them and the conclusions inferred from them, it was this large body of facts
resulting from the long investigation of them by a highly
respected group of outstanding medical scientists that
finally resulted in the condemnation of the serious, widespread habit of cigarette smoking in this country.